Surface To Air System Summer Manual: 2018 Edition

RICH HARGITT

Cover Photo: Brandi Richardson

Diagrams created by Eric Solbakken

Copyright © 2018 Rich Hargitt

ISBN: 1722951192
ISBN-13: 978-1722951191

DEDICATION

This work is dedicated to my wonderful wife, Lisa and our beautiful sons Griffin and Graham. Thanks to my wife for all the endless support in coaching and to my sons for showing me what is really important in this life. Finally, this work is dedicated above all to God who gives me the ability to live each day with strength and honor.
-Rich Hargitt

To my future wife Jessica, thank you for loving me unconditionally. Also, to Lisa, we love you and miss you.
-Eric Solbakken

CONTENTS

1   2x2 RPOs   1

2   3x1 RPOs   18

3   Sniffer RPOs   31

4   QSO   66

5   Locked POP   80

6   3x2 RPOs   85

7   Stick, Snag, Spot, and Motion RPOs   93

FOREWORD

"I am convinced, the way one plays chess always reflects the player's personality. If something defines his character, then it will also define his way of playing." – Vladimir Kramnik undisputed World Chess Champion

2016 was the season. It was the season I decide we had to be different. In a conference full of wing-t and power run teams we were never going to be able to beat the best teams in our conference at their own game. This was not due to lack of toughness by our players but attempting to do so was not going to place our players into a position to be successful. We spent the offseason determined to be not just be a better passing team but the best passing team there was. We worked our tails off. As the season approached something caught my eye.

A coach's Tweets from South Carolina. Film of plays unfolding with a designed fluid chaos pressuring defenses in an assault on all flanks. Tiger Ellison would have been proud and I loved it. I had watched our kids do similar things on their own. It reflected their personalities as players. I reached out to that coach who was kind enough to send me some DVDs and books. I attempted to implement the ideas from my limited resources but shelved the ideas. I knew the ideas would work. I knew also that I was not ready to teach, call and fix those ideas yet. I needed more.

Coach Rich Hargitt was that Coach from South Carolina. I followed his tweets, books, and from time to time I would bug him with an email, text or call. Coach was always happy to help and quick to respond.

In the spring of 2017 I got my chance to begin my formal education in the RPO based offense. It was then Surface to Air (S2A) went live and I jumped at the chance. I learned very quickly how great of a teacher Coach Hargitt is. He packages information in easily learnable chunks that are then used within a module system. This makes it easier for players to learn and recall information quickly while giving the offense a large amount of flexibility. Simple for us. Complex to the defense. Coach Hargitt through experience has crafted the S2A system from the foundation up. I watched Coach as he visited our school lay that foundation from the whiteboard to the practice field. Through the member webinars I got to see Coach Hargitt's thought process during practice leading and its application on game night. It became even clearer that Coach Hargitt was not just a great teacher but a great learner. He was constantly looking for ways to solve problems and improve.

The Surface to Air Summer Manual is a fast resource for S2A members. Answers to questions, seeds to new ideas, and reminders of forgotten coaching points can all be found in its pages. Non S2A members will gain a valuable resource of how to best use formations, personnel, screens and quick game in a RPO offense. As one reads the manual it will be easy to see how these ideas have been crafted to work together to present problems for the defense and answers for the offense.

NonS2A members will also get a glimpse behind the curtain and see what type of information is shared on a regular basis as a S2A member. S2A members from all over the world work closely with each other helping and exchanging ideas daily.

2017 was the season. It was the season we were different. We were not going to shelve the ideas any more. It was like they were playing checkers and we were playing chess. Our team had gained an offseason education in the S2A offense from Coach Hargitt. S2A offense had all the features of all the offenses that I loved growing up. The downhill run game and option of Nebraska to the angle, numbers, and green grass of Kentucky's Air Raid to the play fast, play loose and score mentality of Red Faught's Georgetown College offense. We achieved success like we had never before. We forced teams to change how they played defense. Not just their fronts and coverages but their complete approach to the defensive side of the ball. I don't know if the offense took on our personality or we took on its. I do know we have an identity now. We are different. We are an offense of fluid chaos pressuring defenses in an assault on all flanks.

INTRODUCTION

The purpose of this Surface To Air System Summer Manual is to provide the reader with a basic understanding of what we have attempted to accomplish over the past year in our system. The chapters of this book are a general discussion based upon the webinars that we do on a monthly basis with our members. These webinars are designed to provide insightful commentary and a more broad understanding of an RPO based offense and answer generic and system specific questions that our members may have. This manual is designed to provide not only our members but the general public with a greater understanding of key topics that we feel are instrumental in understanding RPOs in the modern game of football.

This manual is not a complete compilation of all the things that we discussed in a calendar year about the game of football. What this manual is it is a highlight of some of the best points and some of the more insightful commentaries that we have had throughout the year. This manual is designed to inform the reader about some essential and quality topics that we feel should be open to the general public.

We take great pains to answer our members' questions and to keep them constantly informed about the game of football. These webinars are our attempt to provide relevant information to our members on a monthly basis. We look at a variety of topics inside our system and throughout the game of football in general. Some of the topics that we've included for chapters are things that are groundbreaking in our mind such as our QSO section which is based upon the idea of combining quick passes with slow screens into a modern RPO style of play. Some of the other chapters focus on very basic and very rudimentary RPO such as our 2x2 sets that are a basic structure and simple in nature.

I have long been attracted to the idea of taking some of the best thoughts and the best conversations we have throughout the year and offering them to not only our members but to people outside the system as well. When we started the Surface To Air System a year ago we made a commitment that we were a group of football coaches that were committed to helping our members attain more first downs and score more touchdowns. But we also said we are as we are a group of coaches who wanted to see the game of football expand and grow and reach new and healthy heights. Fundamentally we want to see the game of football to improve and to be a safer and a more exciting game. We believe the Surface To Air System is not only making the game safer it is making it more fun. So let's take a look at those two items and break them down separately.

The game of football used to be based out of the wishbone, the wing-t, or the I formation. The game of football used to be a smash mouth concept that utilized very small amounts of the field and a limited amount of creativity to wedge the ball forward a few yards at a time. I played in a system that was fundamentally a smashmouth style of football that lacks creativity and led to a large number of injuries. I can remember being a center and a defensive tackle who obviously played both ways in a small town in Central Illinois. The game was as creative as our coaches could make it at the time. But sadly, the game lacked much imagination outside of the occasional screen, a few deep drop back passes, or even the really exciting occasional bootleg pass. The game, such as it was, was basically a test of wills between the large players just attempting to smash the ball down the field in a very simple and very rudimentary set of plays.

Fortunately, my senior year my high school hired a football coach who began to use some new plays and have some new ideas. When I became a football coach I attempted to follow the model that I had seen for many coaches and I started out running the wing-t. A few years later I became very creative when I started to run the triple-option. Both of these offenses were useful and had stood the test of time. The game was essentially not very safe because what it really consisted of was two football teams lining up basically between the hash marks and proceeding to bludgeon each other down the football field. As I grew in age and in understanding of the game of football I decided that it was time to spread it out and attempt to be more wide-open in our style of attack. Little did I know, but soon began to understand, that when the game is spread out from sideline to sideline and takes on less of a smash-mouth mentality it is also in many cases much safer.

I have begun to notice that as we spread the ball out and we have less of a 3 yards in cloud of dust mentality the number of injuries that we seem to accrue each year has gone down dramatically. While the game of football will never be completely safe, I believe spreading the game out from sideline to sideline and reducing the number of large piles where we have multiple head-on collisions has actually made the game of football much safer.

The second thing the Surface To Air System and other RPO styles of offense has done is it is making the game more exciting. The game of football faces a litany of challenges today and safety is not the only one. Baseball, soccer, basketball, and of course the ubiquitous video games that we see many kids taking time off from high school sports to play are all competing factors in whether or not our young men will continue to pursue the great game of football. Well we hope that football players are multi-sport athletes and we don't wish to make them one sport athletes.

We simply do not want to see them walk away from this great game because those of us that coach it feel that this game is perhaps the one thing that kids might do in their adolescent years that is the greatest purveyor of teamwork known to the coaching profession. This is not meant as an insult to any other sport. Basketball is a team game. Baseball is a team game. But we as football coaches, rightly or wrongly, feel that football is the ultimate team sport. We feel that spreading the football out to a multitude of players and allowing players to play fast and to have fun is going to increase the likelihood that young men will play this sport. When we increase the participation in the sport of football we also increase the participation in a sport that teaches a great deal about life. The more that can be taught and the more values that can be instilled through the game of football we feel like the greater generation of young American men we are able to produce. We feel like the Surface To Air System is then a great motivator to get more kids to want to play football because they will have a better time doing it.

So then what is this manual attempting to accomplish? This manual is attempting to show football coaches how they can instill a greater love of the game of football into their young men by allowing those young man to play a faster and more exciting brand of football. We feel that the Surface To Air System is going to allow kids to play a game that they really enjoy. It is removing the wishbone, wing-t, and I formation slugfest from the mentality and replacing it with a new brand of football that kids in this new century will actually wish to play.

This offense is reflective of what is happening on Saturdays and Sundays at the major college and National Football League levels. The system that we utilize will make more kids want to play the game and will make more kids want to stay with this great game. Therefore, we are attempting to educate coaches on how best to install RPOs so that they can help make the game of football more exciting for the young people that live in their area.

We feel that this manual is a humble contribution to the sport of football. We also hope that this manual sparks in coaches a genuine love of the Surface To Air System as a more modern style of football. We hope that this spark leads to coaches making the game safer and more exciting for their players and thereby increasing participation in the sport. At the time of publication clients in over 30 states in the United States and also in the nations of Brazil, Japan, Canada, and Great Britain have joined the Surface To Air System. We take special pride in attempting to spread the great game of football not only throughout these United States but around the world. As our consultation group grows and we are able to expose our brand of football to more people around the country and around the world we hope that it has a continued and lasting positive effect on the game of football and the people who play it.

This manual, then, is a humble attempt to share some of the values and ideas that we espouse in the Surface To Air System in a text published format for people both inside and outside our system. It is our hope that those coaches who pick up a copy of this manual will soon wish to join our group and help push this great game of football forward. I hope you enjoy the chapters we have selected and I hope the commentary that we share with you is useful to you and helps you in increasing participation in our Sport and in helping the great game of football to move forward!

How do you align to certain formations?

What look do you give the offense?

1

2X2 RPOS

One of the first things that I look at when game planning for an opponent is, how does the defense morph how do they relate to certain formational adjustments, and formational tweaks. What we've never really done is we've never really dug down deep and talked about why you should use it and how you should use it. And what some of the philosophical strategies are behind that. And so that's what we kind of want to dive into in this chapter. Spend a little bit of time on it with you guys.

When you get into a 3x1 set, the defense will have specific rules on how they're going to handle that. What I've noticed, and this is to me a trend over the last few seasons, a lot of defenses don't do very well when you force them to play balanced. So one of the biggest advantages to being in a 2x2 set is, it forces the defense to play balanced. It will, I think, really cut down on their defensive playbook. When I kind of try to go back, I spend a lot of time honestly looking at what defensive coordinators are doing and what some of their ideas are because I think defensive coordinators are really smart guys nowadays.

They have to do a lot of stuff to keep up with us. And I think that they have some really good answers to 3x1. But when I look at what

Reduce the conflict of defenders

those same answers are to 2x2, I don't think that sometimes they're as good of answers. Balancing the defense out, to me, is accomplishing a couple different things. It makes them defend more grass, it makes them defend more diverse areas of grass, it makes them defend balanced areas of grass and we'll talk more about that when get to the diagrams. And it also cuts down on the amount of blitz package they can really throw at you.

I think the next point that's really applicable is, it gives you a true picture. What I mean by that is, when you look at a defense in a 3x1 set, sometimes you really don't know what they're doing because there's a lot of games they can play such as spinning safeties, pulling the rope, bringing a sapper, or bringing a striker. We'll go through what all those terms mean in my Lexicon and what I'm talking about here in just a minute.

If I'm in a balanced 2x2 set, I get a pretty accurate true read of what you're gonna do. If you're a 4-2-5 team and I stand up there and I play a 2x2 and you play two high safeties your will has to either be a box player or he has to be a flat player. If that Will linebacker is trying to be both, he is a RPO coach's greatest dream because I can put him in conflict every single play, every single snap out of 2x2. If you wanna spin a safety down, play six in the box, you're one high all night long. I can go to 3x1 and outnumber you anytime I want. So what 2x2 does, is it allows me to get a true read on you. If you notice on my film a lot of times I'm gonna start you out at 2x2 or in 3x2 because I want to know exactly how you balance up your defense. I wanna start you balanced, and work you to unbalanced. In my opinion, 3x1 is just an unbalanced formation. So that's what I mean by giving you a true read.

The next thing 2x2 gives you a quick setup. A lot of time I call 2x2 right my kids will say all the time, "If we don't see you signal something we just go to 2x2 right." And at practice when every time we go from one drill to the other, the kids will just say, "I wonder if

2

2x2 = Easier to go fast

we're gonna be anything other than 2x2 right." The reason for that is that I default to the Y on the right and the H on the left. I've always done this because I think bubble screen is easier to throw to the quarterback's left so I put the H over there. So if you want to run a lot of plays really, really fast, being a 2x2 team is a great way to get lined up quickly, snap the ball, keep playing, keep using the same formation, stay in a tempo situation.

It doesn't matter where the boundary is. It doesn't matter where the field is if you're in 2x2. You can always just keep getting lined up and decide where front door and back door is to you based upon the concepts. There's a lot of advantages to going fast. There is also an advantage to using 2x2 into a boundary situation and creating a numbers advantage there. So as you take a look at those four things, providing balance and defense, giving us a true read, giving us a quick set up and creating some boundary versus field conflict based on numbers, those are the four things we're looking for and why we're using 2x2.

2x2 RPOs

So let's imagine for a second that we are ball in the middle of the field or maybe ball hugging the left hash just a little bit. I can call inside zone lock to the right. And that grass concept has a lot of room to work over there on the right hand side. Now screen into the boundary is a huge advantage for us. I don't see R2 every trying to be a box player there. I think it's too risky for them. They're probably gonna walk him out (Diagram 1).

Because the L2 is closer to the boundary, is in a great deal of conflict. He knows that he's got the corner out there to help him, but because his hash safety is deeper, he's also gotta be cognizant of the fact that the ball can be thrown into that boundary quickly. He's also got a bubble. He's got a shade five to his side which is an easy place to run the football into. So basically in the S2A, he's a big conflict player.

3

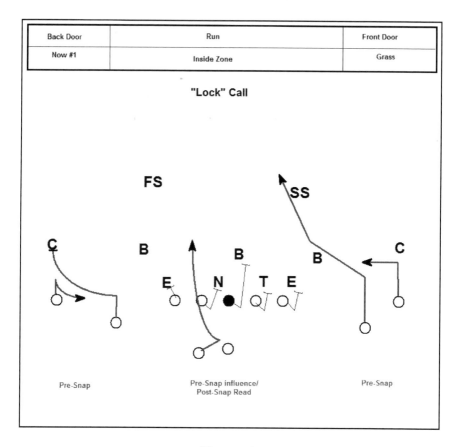

Back Door	Run	Front Door
Now #1	Inside Zone	Grass

"Lock" Call

FS

SS

C   B   B   B   C

E   N   T   E

Pre-Snap   Pre-Snap influence/   Pre-Snap
                  Post-Snap Read

Diagram 1

However, when I go 3x1, he's not nearly inasmuch conflict. They can walk the L3 down, jam the X a little bit on the outside. Roll the L1 down, take away that slant lane a little bit. They can walk the L2 back into the box and they can get an extra half a man at least into the box. So we're assuming this is more your standard 4-2-5 or 43 team.

When I go 2x2, that kid does not have the luxury. If he blitzes, the ball's coming out or the ball's being handed off really doesn't matter. If he comes anywhere near that B gap, we've got numbers into the boundary because we're 2x2 and we're throwing that ball. If he walks all the way out and he wants to cover the H and take him away head up, we're handing the ball off into a five man box. And that's really a big part of what we're trying to do. We're always trying to get back to a five man box so it's one guy for each of our offensive line. And so in this defense with this set, being in 3x1 is not a big advantage for us. But being in 2x2 allows us to create a leverage advantage, and create a conflict defender with the L2 right there.

Now when I talk to my kids, I talk about sappers and I talk about strikers. A striker is like an L2/R2 player in this instance coming off the field side edge. That's a striker to me, usually a front door player. A sapper is a guy coming off the weak side. A lot of defenses like to bring a sapper and the reason that they feel confident in doing that, is they don't feel like you're gonna just throw the ball down here into the boundary because that boundary is their extra defender.

You hear defensive coordinators say it all the time, "We're gonna use the sideline as our extra defender." Okay great. Well here's the deal, my tight end is into the boundary that's the number two receiver. He's gonna go up and block your corner. He's gonna go block your sideline player. And I'm gonna give the ball to my number one receiver down there and I'm gonna let him have all that chunk of grass to work with. If I try to do that out of a 3x1 set, you could very easily just bail that sapper back out, take the slant away and make me play back up to the field.

But by keeping the extra blocker to the boundary, I'm able to create a raw generic numbers advantage. You can see my tight end basically can just bench press that corner into the sideline right there. Now, yes they have a sideline that they can use to their advantage but it's gonna have to be a third level player come get it (Diagram 2).

I don't like that look right there in 3x1 because I don't want to have to throw the ball all the way up there to that wide side. I've created a false numeric superiority for myself down here. Because they've done two things wrong, they've got a corner too far off of a twins set. And they're trying to get pressure.

Back Door	Run	Front Door
Now #1	Inside Zone	Slant

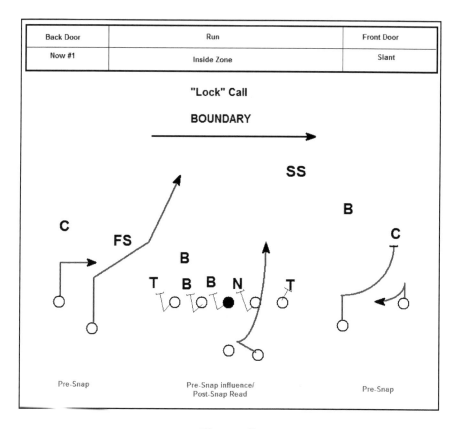

Diagram 2

Now they could very easily take all this problem away. They could take that sapper, go stick him out over number two, walk the corner down, let the safety stay over there and say, "We'll play three over two." My quarterback would never throw that ball into the boundary. The issue is, the box is already somewhat devalued. They've really only got five guys in the box as it is. They're getting their sixth hat with the sapper. So me staying in a 2x2 set right there, is basically just a chance for me to run ISO. It's a pretty darn easy play for me out there.

In the next diagram you will see we are going to lock this play (Diagram 3).

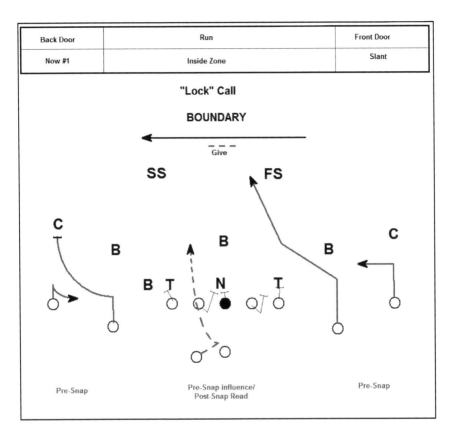

Back Door	Run	Front Door
Now #1	Inside Zone	Slant

"Lock" Call

BOUNDARY

Give

SS   FS

C

B   B

C

B   T   N   T   B

Pre-Snap   Pre-Snap influence/
Post-Snap Read   Pre-Snap

Diagram 3

This look is drawn up against a very standard 3-4 defensive team. You can see the L2 is drawn up trying to be a split the difference guy. If I play 3x1 right there, he is a box player. He will walk down into that B gap, he'll cover the B gap and they'll make me throw front door to the wide side of the field.

Which is fine, and when we get into the 3x1 stuff, we'll talk about how that can be an advantage. But I don't want to do that. I want to throw back door, I want to put that kid in conflict. They're leaving their mic hung out to dry, it's a 4-1 box. I lock the inside zone and I throw Now 1 here. So what they've done is, they've basically balanced their numbers. They've got two guys for my one blocker.

So they've got a free hitter for my X receiver down here. It's fine, the quarterback's not gonna throw the ball down there but he can give his little Brett Favre fake, that's what we call it. He hands the ball off, he gives his little Brett Favre fake. He holds both those defenders.

You can imagine there with that little pitch of his hand, he holds the L3 and the L2 out in the flat. Hands the ball off and it's four down to the Mike now. The greatest run box in history. Four down to the Mike, that's what we want to get every time. Our running back just basically runs through the hole, the Mike might tackle him and he might not but if he tackles him it is five maybe six yards on the other side of the line of scrimmage to our advantage.

This next diagram is one of our one word calls. Let's assume that this ball is in the middle of the field and I am coming out of my own end zone. Now why would I want to be 2x2 here? There's no boundary, there's no field. Why do I decide to use a 2x2 set on say my own one yard line? Let me stop and make a couple points right here. First of all, I'm on my own one yard line and you see what kind of play I'm going to call. I'm going to call an RPO. I'm gonna call a one word RPO. And the reason for that is, and I tell people this all the time, you're good at what you do a lot. That's really the truth about offensive football.

You're good at what you do a lot. I'm not in the I formation a lot, not under the center a lot, I'm not heavy formations a lot because we are not very good at those things. So I'm not gonna get in those on my own one, or on your own one. I'm gonna run what I run well. And what I run well is a quarterback based offense where we read a lot of people.

The reason I'm in 2x2 instead of 3x1 here is I don't want to invite a striker or a sapper. This is a heavy one high defense. Six in the box team. I know for a fact they love to bring pressure when you get into 3x1. Now, normally I'm gonna invite that. I'm fine with that because I want to throw against the pressure. But I don't want to throw against the pressure standing four yards deep in my own end zone, that's not a smart idea. So I stay 2x2, specially from a strategic standpoint so that I know that I've got pretty good chance if they stay six in the box. There's gonna be somewhere for my Quarterback to unload that ball and go get me a first down and get me out of there. So you will see in this next diagram we've got double bubble called here (Diagram 4).

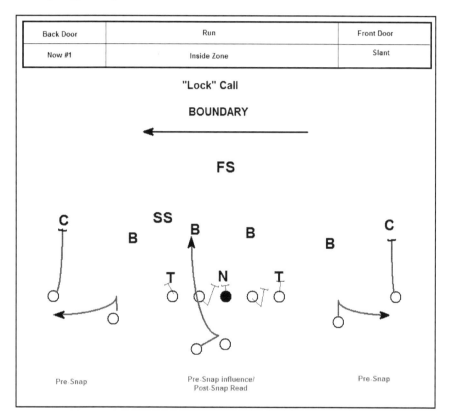

Back Door	Run	Front Door
Now #1	Inside Zone	Slant

"Lock" Call

BOUNDARY

FS

Pre-Snap

Pre-Snap influence/
Post-Snap Read

Pre-Snap

Diagram 4

The Quarterback sees the front door and that the defense didn't cover down the front door receiver very well. We got an angle out there. They tried to cheat a seventh man, or a sixth and a half man into the box. So now you can see we're gonna block their number one. Their number two guy is often times going to be late to the party. He'll still get out there and be involved in the tackle but by the time he gets there, my H receiver's already got the ball. He's out of the end zone and now instead of standing four yards deep in my own in zone, I'm up at the seven, eight, nine yard line.

Now I've got the cushion that I need to be able to go play. That is a strategic decision. That is a decision based upon the idea I don't want to invite a blitz there and through film study and through experience in this game, I felt like being in 3x1 in my own in zone would invite pressure from them. So that was the safest way for me to avoid that pressure.

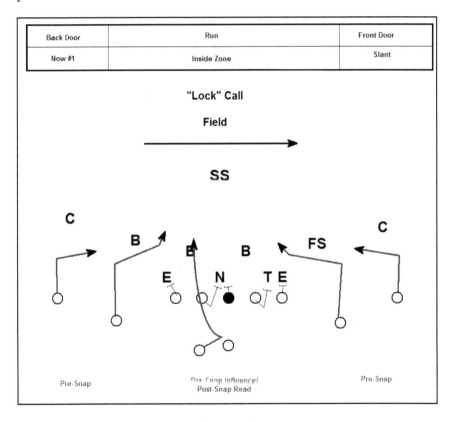

Back Door	Run	Front Door
Now #1	Inside Zone	Slant

Diagram 5

The field and boundary might dictate a reason that I want to be 2x2, I might want to invite more front door slants. We will assume in this next diagram that the defense plays a 4-2-5 defense and that they play six in the box (Diagram 5).

So I'm expecting the weak safety to roll down and rob that and for them to play a 4-4 defense basically. I want the quarterback to get more front door throws. So if I stay 2x2, I feel like I'm gonna have more opportunity to get to the front door. If I'd have gone 3x1 right there, I don't feel like I get that. I feel like they pulled the rope all the way over, they take it away. We pitch it, we catch it, we get an easy first down.

So sometimes it may be as simple as if I wanna throw more front door grass, I may need to stay in 2x2 more even when I'm on the hash. I've been around coaches before that they'll tell me they'll say, "Well every single time I get on a hash mark, I'm gonna go trips to the field. That's just my thinking, I'll go 2x2 if the ball's in the middle but on a hash I always go 3x1."

I just don't agree with that, I understand why people do that, I understand how sometimes that can be an advantage. But sometimes it's not. I want to throw front door grass right there and by not having a third receiver in the way, I've created a big patch of grass where I can work that ball into. So if you're having a lot of trouble getting to the front door slant, that's a great way to get to it.

Against a 3-3 stack defense it is also sometimes preferable to stay in a 2x2 structure if you want to work to the front door side of the field. 3-3 teams do not like to break the stack, they will not break the stack. They will always want to keep six in the box. By keeping six in the box, I can play front door grass anytime I want (Diagram 6).

If I go 3x1 they will start to either nipple that strong stack out, or they'll roll the free safety down and camp him out over number three and they'll make me play more back door. We manufacture that grass. You can see there, by staying 2x2 to me, you're really just running an inside seem is what it amounts to.

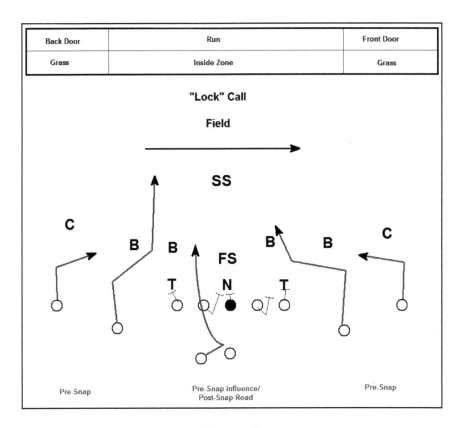

Back Door	Run	Front Door
Grass	Inside Zone	Grass

"Lock" Call

Field

SS

C
B   B   FS
T   N   T

B   B   C

Pre-Snap   Pre-Snap influence/   Pre-Snap
                  Post-Snap Read

Diagram 6

That's a ball we can throw because we're staying in that 2x2 set. So I think that's something you gotta be cognizant of. People ask me sometimes they'll say, "Well how do I get more front door throws?" Play more 2x2. If you're in 2x2 more, you'll get more front door throws.

The other thing is, go 3x1 to the front door side and you'll get more front door throws. So it's kind of you can manufacture them, sort of how you want. And that's sort of what we do, is we kind of go through and find out when we haven't gotten enough of them lately. We'll just manufacture them and sort of put them in there where we want them.

Now let's say you want to run stick. The stick for us in the Surface

To Air System is fade by one, flat by two, hitch by three if he was there. Stick from 3x1 is a great play but we are focusing on how and why we want to run Stick from a 2x2 set. I sometimes feel like it is a much cleaner read for us to play out of 2x2. Which I think is a great point for those of you that are running this type of stuff for the very first time.

My new Quarterback in Idaho was in the I formation last year and had no experience with RPOs. We'll start him out with a lot of 2x2 RPOs because I feel like the picture is much cleaner when you're in a 2x2 that it is when you're in 3x1. I think you're able to read things a lot easier. And your picture's much clearer than it is when you start adding that third receiver. So in this next diagram (Diagram 7).

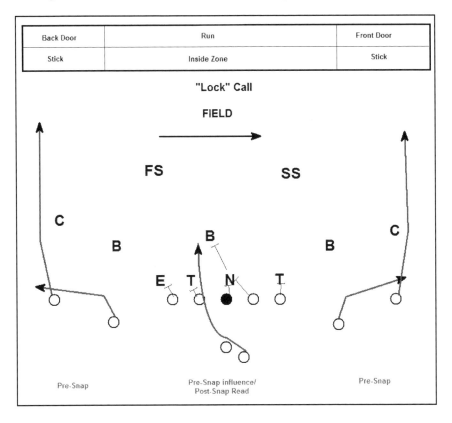

Back Door	Run	Front Door
Stick	Inside Zone	Stick

Diagram 7

The R2 defender is inside of our wide receiver.

So it's pretty easy money the quarterback knows right now based upon leverage he can throw that. That corner has no safety help over the top so you will see the corner bail pretty often. The quarterback knows this is an easy flat throw versus this type of coverage. The Quarterback is able to just pitch and catch with that leverage and it is easier to read for the quarterback because he doesn't have a third receiver, he doesn't have a third defender in there. A lot of people don't think that 2x2 RPOs are as extravagant as 3x1 RPOs but they're very simple and they're simple for a reason and they work for a reason.

Next let's turn to the taper fade concept (Diagram 8).

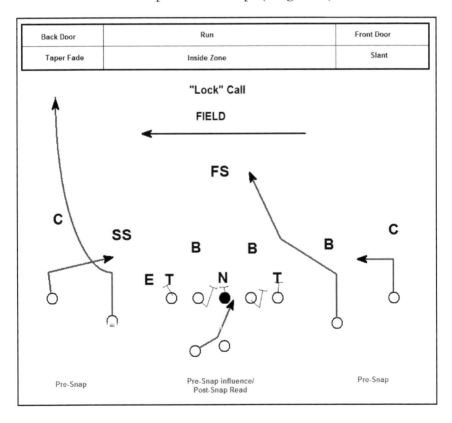

Diagram 8

So two is gonna run the taper fade, everybody in college football wants to call it the slot fade. We've been run it for four, five years I never knew it was called a slot fade until I watch Sports Center. Our number one is going to run a stutter slant. So he's gonna push up a couple steps, he's going to kind of jitterbug the outside shoulder of that L3 defender and then come on a slant underneath and read the grass.

Now why do I do this out of 2x2? Well I need to identify the coverage. And to me, if you're in 2x2 it's very hard to disguise your coverage. Everybody says, "Oh man, 3x1 I can't disguise my coverage but 2x2 I can't." I don't understand that. 2x2 if it's done right, is a hard coverage to disguise against.

I've got both receivers outside the hash if the ball is in the middle of the field. So this is 2x2 wide to us meaning I've widen them out a little bit. And so I've got the coverage identified. In this case, if they are in Cover 1, then the free safety is sitting dead red in the middle of the football field, he's not a factor.

We're running a fade down the numbers from our number two receiver. That safety's never gonna get there. So that's another reason why you might want to stay in 2x2 because I feel like sometimes you tip the defenses hand a little bit and you force them to give you an answer that they otherwise would not give you.

There are also several good reasons to stay in a 2x2 set down on the goal line. When you get down here in a red zone situation and you go trips, you invite the sapper, you invite the striker. It's hard to sometimes tell with all those bodies down there what coverage they're in. So if you put them in 2x2 it's a much easier coverage to understand. This is one of our goal line plays. We have six options (Diagram 9).

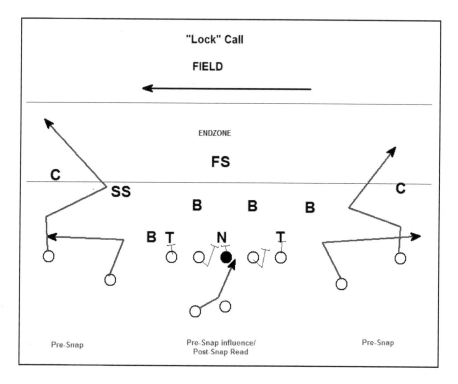

"Lock" Call

FIELD

ENDZONE

FS

C

SS

B   B   B

B T   N   T

C

Pre-Snap   Pre-Snap Influence/   Pre-Snap
                  Post-Snap Read

Diagram 9

We have two over here on the right, two on the left. And the quarterback decides to either hand it to the running back or to keep it himself. He has run or pass options to his side and the running back has the same run to pass options if he is given the ball on his side. This sort of play balances the defense and requires them to play the formation honestly.

Conclusion

Defenses have said they are going to become very complicated in the way in which they attempt to attack offenses. It is up to the offensive play-caller to find the best ways to attack defenses as the game continues to evolve at a rapid rate. Often times a 3x1 structure makes it much easier for the defense to mutate themselves into a situation that is advantageous for them to be competitive. A 2x2 structure will oftentimes force the defense to play balanced and thereby take away many of the different types of blitzes that they want to utilize in a specific game plan. A good play caller should always attempt to use a wide variety of formations however many times the 2x2 structure has been under-utilized in the game of football as more people rush to employ empty sets and 3x1 structures.

It is necessary to utilize 2x2 structures in any game plan because by nature these structures force the defense to not only be balanced but they also give the offense a boundary to field component. Many defenses are attempting to shift their resources towards the wide side of the field and by staying in a 2x2 structure the offense is able to countermeasure that type of idea. While 2x2 structures may be one of the oldest ways that spread offenses were designed it is still one of the more effective ways to do so and while 3x1 structures certainly have their place the 2x2 style of offense should still be utilized and still be a major part of your offensive game plan.

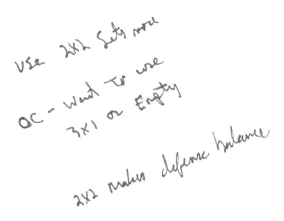

Use 2x2 Sets more

OC - Want to use 3x1 or Empty

2x2 makes defense balance

2

3X1 RPOS

When I look at the RPO, when I look at defenses I look at it the same way that a general should look at a battlefield. I'm gonna move this piece, when I move this piece what are you gonna do? If I don't know the answer to that, and I don't already know what my next move is then I'm not doing a very good job as an offensive coordinator. I have to guess one step ahead of you. I have to anticipate your reaction to my action. If not, I'm a defensive coordinator. That's what the defensive coordinator's doing. He is reacting to an action. I am making the action, but when I make the action I'm already guess what your reaction is. And I'm trying to move the chess piece one step further ahead. That's how you get more first downs and more touchdowns in my position.

So now everything we just said about 2x2 in the first chapter is 100% true. But there is a reason to get into 3x1. And honestly we could have a whole chapter on why you should get into 3x2 which I think is not a combination of 3x1 and 3x2 at all. It a whole 'nother animal but our purpose in this chapter is to discuss 3x1. So in 3x1 you get to tip the defenses hand. In 2x2 to me, you prevent them from blitzing, you prevent them from changing coverage. You prevent the defense from getting outside their comfort zone. You make them play base. So if you want them to play base, play a lot of 2x2 RPOs. If you do not want them to play base and you want to see what tricks they have up their sleeve, go to 3x1. Because in 3x1 you're going get them to tip their hand and they're going change some stuff and they're going to bring some wrinkles out of that playbook. Why would you want to do this? Well, if you want them bring the sapper because you think you can hammer them on the weak side, there you go. If you want them to bring the striker because you think the front door side you can do some damage, there you go. If you want them to roll to one high and cover you down and give you mono-e-mono on your best receiver, then God be with you. There are some reasons why you'd want to do it. I do it, I'll go 2x2 for a couple plays or I'll go 3x2 for a couple plays to start the game. After I have assessed the defense then I'll switch you over and I'll put you in 3x1 because I want to see what your answer is there too. And to be quite honest, I want to see as a defensive coordinator have you done your homework? How much have you done your homework? How much have you studied me that week? Have you really ruined your Sunday by sitting there and charting out everything I'll do out of those two formations. And if you haven't, let's go ahead and get some cheap first downs and get the ball moving right now.

The next thing is do they have a one on one dude? Everybody says they do, everybody says well we got a guy that can play one on one on their best receiver. All right, well let's find out. Let's find out right by God now. Let's find out that first series. Do you really have a guy that will walk down in the X receiver's face, press him up on his inside shoulder, and play man all night long everywhere he goes? If you do, my next question is do you have a guy inside of him that can man my running back up? Because I'm gonna slant you, and wheel you. I'm gonna post you and wheel you. I'm gonna spot and wheel you. I'm gonna do all kinds of stuff to that weak side to find out, do you really have two guys can play man coverage on that weak side. I love listening to DCs they will all tell you, "Oh we're just gonna play cover zero on half the field and overload the trip side and we're gonna win." I'm like, "All right." But you give up one slant, that things going to run all day. And we all know that. I can run an under route and a wheel route and your linebacker can't cover the running back. It's just exactly the same as my X can't be covered by your corner it's the same problem.

I think you need to find that out about the defense and I think you need to find it out early. The next thing 3x1 does is it causes a box manipulation. They have to decide to cover these three receivers over here, and how to matriculate and manipulate the second level of the defense to make sure that the box is still sound. And some people can't do that. And some people can't do it fast. And some people can do it but their 16 year old Mike linebacker can't get it called fast enough. So you need to figure that out and you need to see how much damage you can do there.

The other great thing 3x1 does, is it causes a ton of L2/R2 manipulation. You can do a lot of stuff to those two guys out of 3x1. When you manipulate them, you're also doing it to the safeties because they have to clean up the mess of wherever the L2 and the R2 are moving. If L2's coming on a sapper blitz off that back door weak side, great but what's L1 doing? Is L1 got the back? Is L1 playing over the top coverage and they're trapping the corner? Whatever L2 and R2 do, L1, R1 have to do the same symbiotic thing with the defense. So I think that's really important you understand, you are stressing those guys out across the board. And I think that's an important thing to be able to do in 3x1.

3x1 RPOs

If you look at this 4-4 defense, they have a fundamental issue (Diagram 10).

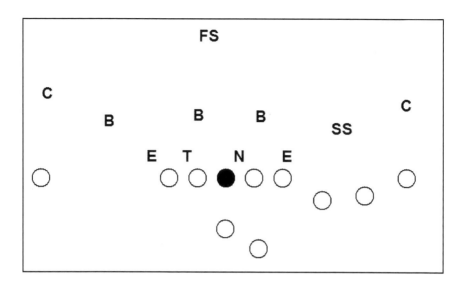

Diagram 10

Do they pull the rope? Now when I say pull the rope, that means do they take one of those linebackers and move him out to cover the #3 receiver? So if that left Mike is going be a rope pull, he's gonna go all the way outside that defensive end that we're reading and he's gonna go stand out there and apex the H and the defensive end. The right Mike is going be in the left A gap where the left Mike is. And the R2 is going to walk in and cover the B gap.

If they do that, you should play one on one with your Z receiver all night long even if it means getting out of the RPO game. If they don't do that, you can throw the ball to the bubble all night long. If they attempt to do something else like bring the number one down and cover up and play zero, either get out of the RPO game and play PAP or block drop back and strike them.

Another answer is to just play zone read football because you got five for five and you're still reading the defensive end. But you have forced a manipulation and a defense. They cannot just sit in that 4-4 Cover 3 and say, "We're good." You're not good. The defense is double teaming the slant and you're two over three on the bubble right now. My quarterback should throw the ball to that bubble screen over and over and over and over again right now. You have to change your defense when I go 3x1. Now, the whole reason we have the 2x2 conversation is, if I don't want you to change it because I like the way you're setting in base and I want to attack you then I stay in 2x2. If I want you to change it because I want to manipulate you and I think your change is gonna give me an advantage, then I should be playing 3x1.

The next play we will look at is a one word RPO so we're going really, really fast (Diagram 11).

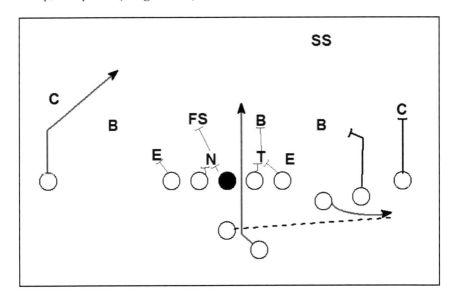

Diagram 11

Why is this applicable? If you line up fast, most teams will worry about protecting the box and then they figure out the split receivers later. It takes them a second to realize they should probably send one more guy out there to cover three. That's a pre snap look, the Quarterback will just dip that ball and sling it out there. Good things are gonna happen to us out there on the perimeter. So we throw that ball out there and that's likely going to be a first down right there.

Next let's look at 3x1 into the boundary. Why do you we trips into the boundary? We're shoving all kinds of people up into that boundary. I want you to imagine, take the center and let's draw a line at the center. I know we're on a short field, how many people are on the wide side of the field from the center?

There are three and a half people covering basically half, a little more than half the football field. So let's give it four, let's say it's the full four. Well I've shove seven people over into the boundary by putting trips into the boundary side in the shorter side of the field. Now it's just an easy hand off in the B gap. Nobody fills and that kid takes off and gets a 15, 16 yard run. That's why we run the ball so effectively is because we manipulate the defense. We're trying to think one step ahead. And what we had seen there, is when we go trips to the boundary a lot of times we're forcing that defense to shove itself over there (Diagram 12).

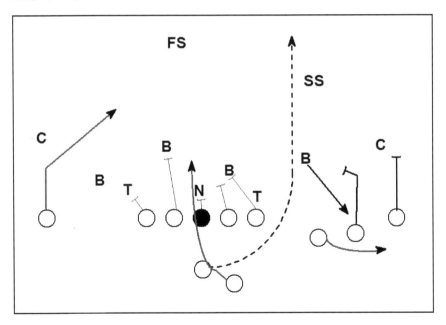

Diagram 12

Many times it is necessary to manipulate these 3x1 sets in order to find out where the defense is giving me numbers. If I set 3x1 to the field I'm not blocking the defense end. This formation gives me a running back, quarterback, and three receivers to one side of the field and so there's a lot of good things gonna happen to me with that formation set to the field. In this instance the defense is outnumbered because I have four and they only have three players (Diagram 13).

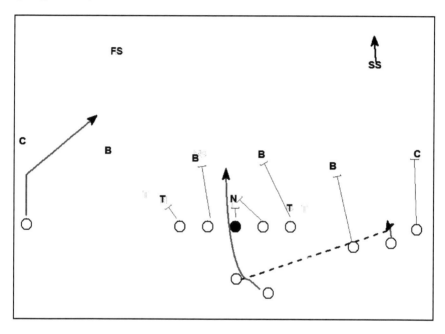

Diagram 13

And that's really what the RPO game is it is getting the football to where the numbers advantage is in favor of the offense. And we did that with the formation. We put ourselves in a situation where there is a high probability of success.

I love when people talk about the say, "Well you all don't play power football," "You don't play power football in the RPO game." "Yes we do, we just moved it 20 years yards away from the center." So if you look I've got three receivers into the boundary, they've got two defenders; one covering my number one receiver, one covering my number three receiver, nobody covering my number two receiver.

If we just throw it to the number two guy, you've got an ISO. You've got full backs on two linebackers, you got a tailback with the ball in his hands and the linebacker's gotta come from 13 yards deep to tackle. All I have do is get to 10 yards before the safety does. 3x1 into the boundary is something that many defenses don't like because it forces them to distort their coverages in ways they don't like.

The next diagram is 3x1 to the field. This is Inside zone with triple hitches, meaning defenders can't cover both of these plays and maintain two high safety structures (Diagram 14).

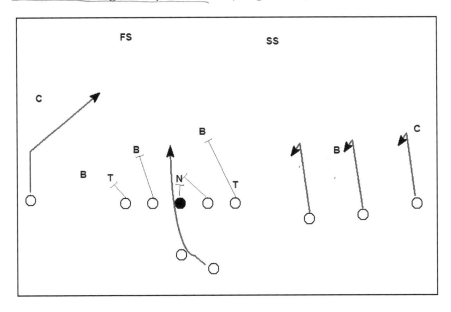

Diagram 14

There's only one guy to cover the two hitches so we tell the quarterback, "If the first hitch is open, throw it. If they cover the first hitch, go to the next hitch. If they cover that hitch go to the next hitch." Don't make it hard just throw the first open hitch you've got. So that's pretty easy football but it's easy football because of the 3x1 to the field structure.

Now, we run a fair amount of Bubble Screens when we are in 3x1 sets. So there are times where we want to run slant bubble. We design this play for when the defense would want to jump the bubble hard. So we would likely put 3x1 to the field knowing that it's a long run for the L2/R2 player and we can bring the wide receiver, the number two behind him on a slant (Diagram 15).

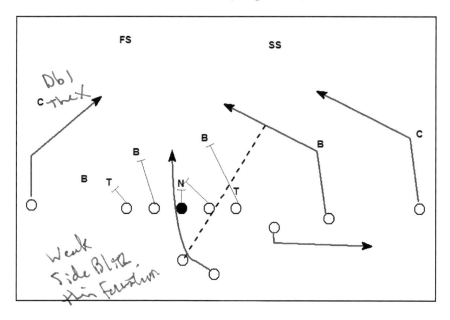

Diagram 15

This is a locked inside zone and the Mike is coming down and is likely going to be a heavy run player and we are assuming they are going to jump the bubble. This will make for an easy pitch and catch. All that stuff is engineered by using the formation and putting the formation in a situation that is to our advantage.

A common answer by a lot of defenses is to utilize a weak side outside linebacker on a blitz which is what we in Surface To Air call a Sapper. This sort of technique will inspire us to utilize more 3x1 to the field in the especially in the second half of games because we found out it invites the blitz. Well every time it invites the blitz there corner is no match for our Z. That's usually a matchup advantage for us. So we know that pretty often we will get bail coverage and most defenses don't want to play man to man over there. So we know any kind of slant, hitch, out, now screen basically any kind of quick game we want to run, we could throw it over there all night long (Diagram 16).

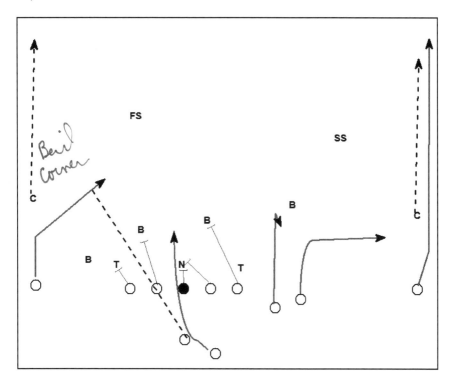

Diagram 16

Another way to accomplish this is to call inside zone lock and utilize a Snag Concept to the field. We can call 3x1 to the field and run the inside zone back into the boundary side of the field and control the blitz weak and aid in running the ball in the box. A lot of Cover 4 or quarters type teams will basically end up almost triple teaming our single receiver. They will end up with an R3, R2 and the R1 all accounting for that one guy. They're overcompensating to the single receiver side because they like to bring pressure from that side when you show 3x1. We can go lock and when we call that the back is automatically bending into the back door side (Diagram 17).

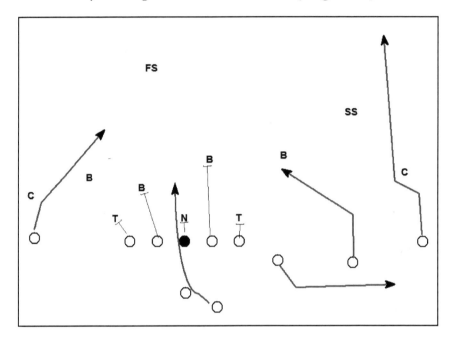

Diagram 17

So we're basically ignoring all those defenders up there to the front door side. We know we can lock that ball and run it back into the back door side.

In this final clip we are looking at 3x1 to the field against a quarters look.

So the only way we could get that was putting trips to the field. In this last diagram we are looking at a post snap pull read so let's assume the dive back is taken away and the quarterback will be pulling the ball and attacking the perimeter. We are executing the Spot Concept with a corner route by the number two receiver, bubble by number three, and spot by number one (Diagram 18).

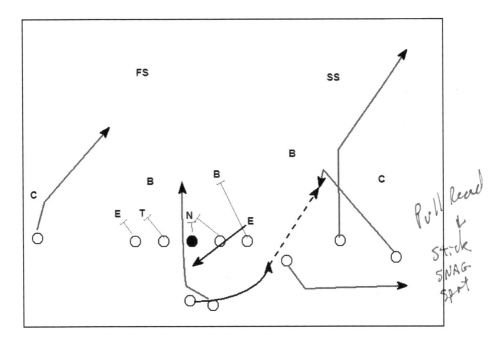

Diagram 18

When we feel that we will get a pull read we like to run a stick, a snag, or a spot concept out wide and really attack the L2/R2 player and gain huge chunks of yardage out there off the pull. The route depths allow for easy throws but also keep defender sin grass if the quarterback should want to keep the ball and attack the flank of the defense.

Conclusion

2 x 2 sets and 3x1 sets are both critical to utilize in today's modern spread offenses. A coach as a play caller must determine whether 2 x 2 or 3x1 are the better way to attack a defense. In many cases the answer is to use both of these formations equally and to try to attack the defense from a variety of different looks. While a 2x2 set might be a great way to balance the defense up the 3x1 set is actually a great way to invite the blitz and attack the blitz should that be the type of defense you are seeing. The 3x1 set is a great way to outflank and manipulate the L2/R2 defender that most defenses prioritize in

bringing different types of pressure schemes and disguising their defenses.

3 x 1 set should be evaluated and monitored week by week to determine how and when it best attacks modern defenses. It is up to the play-caller to determine whether or not this formation should be the basis of the attack that week or whether it should be a changeup. Regardless of whether 3 x 1 is utilized a large amount or a small amount it is a pivotal and crucial piece of the puzzle in being a productive surface-to-air style offense.

L2/R2 defender is a blitz trigger

3x1 = Basis of offense or change-up

3
SNIFFER RPOS

What we're here to discuss in this chapter is our version of the sniffer tight end in the Surface to Air System. So when we talk about Sniffer RPOs, obviously we're talking about to us, is the Y receiver being in the backfield in some situation. There's a lot of things that I think happens to defenses when they have to prep for a sniffer, and most of those things are not good for the defense. Most of them are advantageous for the offense. We think using an in line tight end has become a bit antiquated and have not used it much. Instead we have evolved to the sniffer because we feel like that guy's able to do more while the traditional tight end is only able to do certain things. He's able to block the guy in front of him, he's able to block down, he's able to runner out to the flat, or he's able to runner out vertically. So there's a lot more that can go into that, there's a lot more that the sniffer can do. We talk about there being really five major things that makes a sniffer advantageous in the S2A. The first one is that it changes the structure. It changes the structure of the offense, which thereby forces the defense to change their structure. The second thing it does is it creates an extra gap. It's generally creating an extra gap somewhere out there that the defense cannot prep for (Diagram 19).

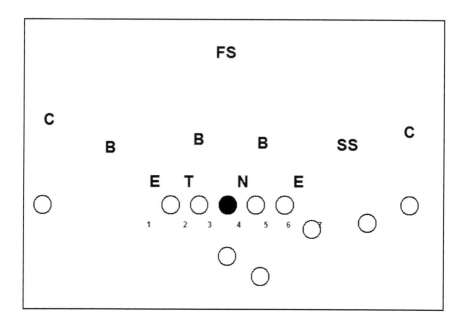

Diagram 19

When you put the sniffer to the right, let's say, you're creating that extra gap to the right, but because the sniffer can also trade across the formation, he can split zone, he can load option across, it's creating that extra gap in a multitude of places. It might be on the right where he lines up, but it could be all the way across the other side of the formation, and that's one of the things we really like is it creates both a front door, and a back door gap. It also allows us to split and load option the defense, which we will get to later. It allows us new ways to attack the grass, and it allows us to attack new places in the defensive structure.

That's something we felt like we were missing before we started using the sniffer. And the last big component is it allows us to isolate defenders, and it allows us to aide in the triple option. So I think gone are the days where we are just gonna sit around, and play with an in line tight end, we still do it from time to time, but the majority of our tight end formations now involve that sniffer. That is a huge answer when people play man coverage, or when they try to do some funky things to us defensively.

So if you have that sniffer tight end on the right side in my opinion is able to split zone the defensive in front of him, he is able to load option around, and block the linebacker above the C gap, he's able to insert. That's three things he can do on his side, then he can do the same three things crossing the formation, that gives him six options. He's also able to pop pass on his side, that's seven. He can go to the flat, that's eight, or he can boot all the way across to the other side of formation, that's nine. So there's nine different things that Sniffer allows us to do, and change the surface of our offense up pretty significantly. That causes the defense to have to process out a lot of different changes that we get to manipulate throughout the structure of the offense, and as I said before, when we start to get a lot of man coverage teams, or we get teams that want to change gaps on us like 3-3 teams the sniffer's an almost guaranteed go to answer.

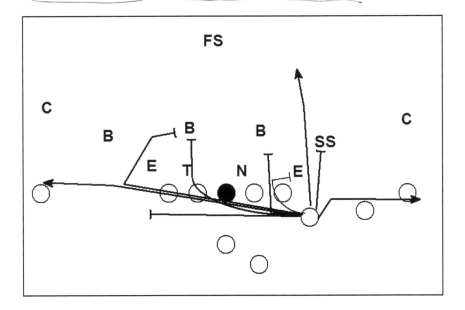

Diagram 20

So when you look at this next diagram here at the effects of the sniffer, you get a lot of crazy answers to that guy being out there, and one thing that I think is important to stop, and really discuss right here is defenses all identify the sniffer differently (Diagram 20).

In practice every day our defensive coordinator declared me to be in two back. Now I see nothing about the Sniffer being a two back set. I'm not in two backs, I don't mean to be in two backs, I never got to hand it to that guy, but I hear defenses all the time declare that to be two backs. That is an 11 personnel offense to me, always has been, always will be. But a lot of defensive coordinators don't see it that way so they immediately go to what their two back answer is. You can see this team time in practice a lot. The defense is going to often have a standard answer to any kind of two back set which is to bring another hat into the box, and roll the strong safety down. So you can see the strong safety over there, the R1 has come down on the slot, and they've moved the R2 into the box to create a four three look. That all sounds fine, well, and good, but the issue here is that I'm gonna throw the ball over here to the front door side to this single side receiver slant.

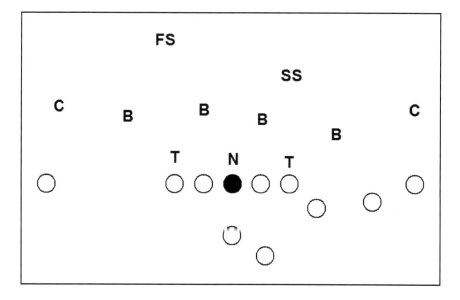

Diagram 21

They've created a false grass area, they've created a large patch of grass where there should not be one. And so by employing the Sniffer, and moving the Sniffer around into both a 2x2 and a 3x1 surface you're able to really manipulate the defense and manipulate what the edges of the defense are gonna look like.

Now let's look at a diagram of a standard 3-4 defense and how they will normally treat it as two backs in the box (Diagram 21).

They will bring their L2 down into the box. They have some serious numbers issues now to the 3x1 side. One of the most advantageous things we do with the sniffers, we put them in the game just to set an edge, and run outside zone out of. Once we're able to run outside zone outside of the Sniffer, the defense has to mutate in order to figure that out. They've gotta walk an extra hat down there, and realize that there's not just an A, a B, and a C gap, but there's an A, B, C, and a D gap. Once they do that, and they make their required adjustments to that, it opens up a whole host of other things we're gonna talk about tonight that you're able to do with that sniffer.

Sniffer- Run outside Insert   *Create the Extra gap*

Sniffer Insertion

Next let's take a look at when we have got an insertion by the tight end. The defense recognizes that tight end as a threat to create an extra gap outside, and we've probably run outside zone on them multiple times. What they're not prepared for, is they're not prepared for that tight end to be an insert guy, and for it to be an iso block on the back door side right there (Diagram 22).

And so that's what I mean, once you set them up by adding that extra gap outside to run outside zone, which we did several times to this sort of team, you're now able to insert that guy, or you're able to bring him across the formation and start adding gaps inside the box. And that's one of the things I love about sniffers, you really get to decide whether you're gonna add that extra gap outside the box, or whether you're gonna add that extra gap inside the box. I think that's a pretty critical component to what we're trying to do with that formation.

Defenses are going to play four down most of the time when they see you put that sniffer in the game because they're either identifying you as an 11 personnel team, or they're identifying you as a two back team. Most of the people in South Carolina identify me as a two back offense once they see the sniffer in the game, and it's perfect because I know what I'm going to get.

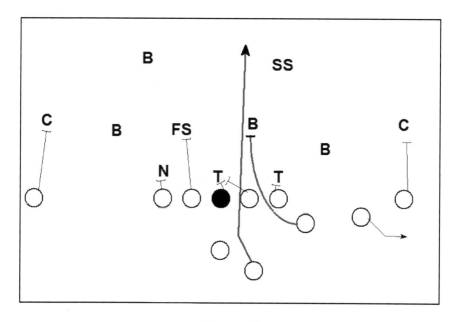

Diagram 22

I'm going to get that extra walk down, and they're basically playing a seven man front. They can't leave my H receiver uncovered because he's one of the best receivers I've got, so where do you get an honest and easy answer? Over there on the front door side. You almost always get big, and easy grass throws to the front door side from a sniffer set. It is that sort of distortion that makes your sniffer sets that much more lethal for the defense to process out. It's just a shell game like we're always playing, and it's an opportunity basically to add one hat where they're not prepared to have it show up. And I think that's really the big advantage to using a sniffer instead of an in line tight end because that in line tight end cannot split zone, he cannot insert, he can't do some of those things as easily to change the numerical superiority in the box or at the edges of the box.

Some defenses will just roll down into a seven man front, once they get down into a seven man front there's lots of grass over here to the front door side it doesn't take a lot of experience to be able to execute this route now, three steps, and run to the grass. The quarterback can have an easy pitch and catch (Diagram 23).

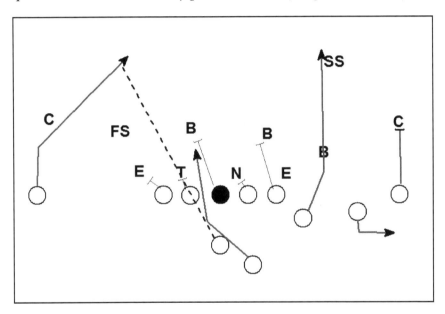

Diagram 23

Distorting The Defense With The Sniffer

The beauty of that sniffer being involved is whoever the guy is behind the defensive end, and the defensive end himself are always in a question mark state, not really knowing what they're gonna get. Are they gonna get hooked? Are they gonna get kicked? Are they gonna get read? There's something happening to the flank, to the edge of that defense on every play, and those two players, the five technique, and the linebacker directly behind the five technique never know which permutation I'm gonna throw at them until the ball is snapped.

Those are the things to me, that you need to train your quarterback up first and foremost, is to make sure that he always takes advantage of the front door grass every time you're in any kind of 3x1 sniffer set. Now when you go to 2x2 sniffer, it creates a whole host of other issues for the defense on their balance and how they have to handle all that stuff. So basically what we're talking about now is what happens when you put that sniffer in the game to establish field and boundary tendencies. So here we're assuming that the field is to the right side. We've got the sniffer to the wide side of the field, and so the R2 is going to have to set that edge.

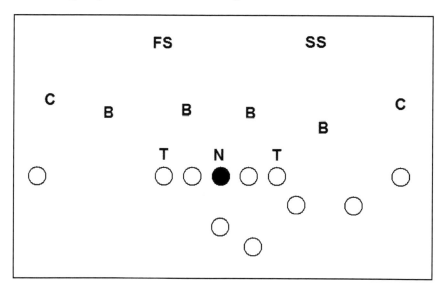

Diagram 24

They do not want to be out flanked over there, so they have to keep the R2 as the D gap player. They're almost forced to play a five technique at the bare minimum to take the C gap, and they have to have a backer, and they have to have the R3. Unless they're going to play straight lock down man coverage, this formation is almost forcing the defense into a two high shell (Diagram 24).

So if you're getting a lot of one high, and you want to get them back into two high, a great way to do that is to play out of 2x2 sniffer. One of the things we really like to do, is we like to add stack sets back into the boundary. So in this next image I'm stacking the H behind the X, and I'm now asking the L2, what do you want to do? Do you want to go out and cover the stack? Or do you want to be a box player? You immediately have to declare, and there's really no hiding that (Diagram 25).

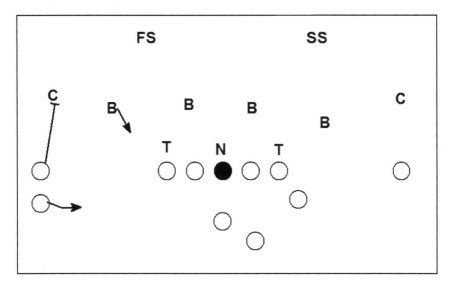

Diagram 25

I already know what the tight end set is going to look like over on the other side because I know how you have to adjust to tight end split, but because I've kept the formation balanced I'm almost forcing you to play two high, and when we're in this formation we get almost exclusive two high looks out of this. I'm not exactly sure unless you're gonna play 3-3 stack, how you want to get into a one high look right here. The beauty of it is, if you get into one high 3-3 stack, I'll bring the sniffer from the right back to the left, I'll load option, and split you, and I'll always have a one hat advantage back to the weak side. So this is just another classic example of using formations to get what you want using the sniffer.

I'm predicating what look I know I'm going to get right here, and I'm pretty confident L2 is going to hang in between, and he's going to at the last second have to make a declaration to either play the box, or to play the stack set. I have shown the defense a 2x2 set, and I've gotten them to play balanced defense, but by bringing the sniffer from the right back to the left, and utilizing that stack set, I've put the defense into a 3x1 set late.

I've made them defend a 3x1 set at the snap of the ball. I just didn't let him see it and declare it. If I would've lined up with the 3x1 sniffer over here, they would've rolled the one high safety, and they would've balanced the numbers. By splitting the tight end from the wide side back to the boundary side, I'm able to create the numbers I want, and I'm able to create it post snap, and put that situation out there where I want it to be.

Many defenses prefer to play squeeze/scrape against modern zone read and RPO teams. Squeeze/scrape to a sniffer set to me is a dead entity. It's almost impossible to do that right if I have all of those conflicting options available to me. If I'm able to split, load, throw arrow, throw pop, and insert, if all those things can happen I think squeeze/scrape is a dead act against the sniffer set. And so whenever I see people trying to squeeze/scrape me out of 2x2 or 3x1, I put the sniffer in the game, gash them a couple times, and we move on.

The great thing about defenses are they usually come into every game with one or two main RPO killing ideas, and if squeeze/scrape is all you brought to the party the sniffer set can set you up for a good night because the defense is going to have to go to a secondary option. If you've worked all those squeeze/scrape techniques all week, and my sniffer can erase those things you're automatically on plan B. It's been my experience, defenses don't operate very well on plan B.

If the defense elects to line up a player over the sniffer then that is a conflict player.

They've got four down and they've got three linebackers in the box. With the sniffer being there, that third linebacker who's walked down on the tight end, he really never has a clue what's happening to him. I can kick him out, I can block him, I can pop him, I can flat him, I can insert, and leave him out there and read him (Diagram 26).

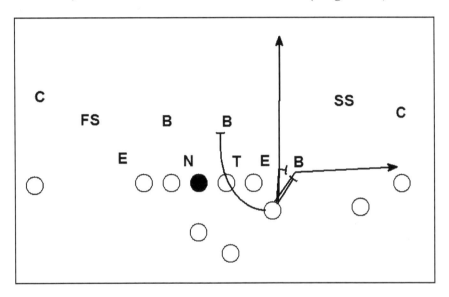

Diagram 26

He's in a really bad way, and if I was just in 3x1 and had a split receiver out there instead of a sniffer he would be able to dictate a multitude of answers to me. He'd be able to decide when he's gonna feather, when he's gonna bring pressure, when he's gonna wall number three, when he's gonna man number three, he would be able to provide a bunch of different question marks for my quarterback to read. But when I have a Sniffer in the game I have that dry erase marker last. I have the ability to put him in conflict in a bunch of different ways, and try to make his life stressful.

POP Passes

Most of the time when we're running POP with number three, we're playing some sort of two man game with you with two of our other receivers. In this next diagram we are running a Spot and a Bubble Route with our two wide receivers (Diagram 27).

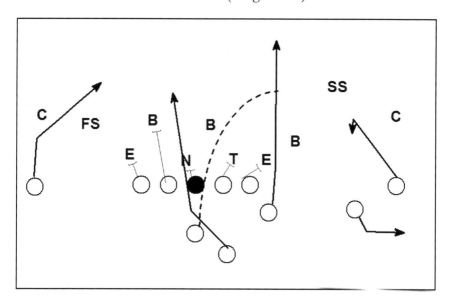

Diagram 27

All we're trying to do there is we're trying to pull two of your three defenders away from the box and erase them on the perimeter. The R1, R2, and R3 are all likely to be influenced by these two receivers. The grass may not have to be 15, 20 yards down the field. In this case, it's three yards behind the defensive end, but that's where the defense has chosen to leave themselves vulnerable. And I think that's a key game planning coaching point is we all need to start to realize defenses are not as mercurial as they think they are. They always leave gaps in their structure. They always have vulnerabilities in their structure. Sometimes you can see defenses are completely screwed up because of this tight end set (Diagram 28).

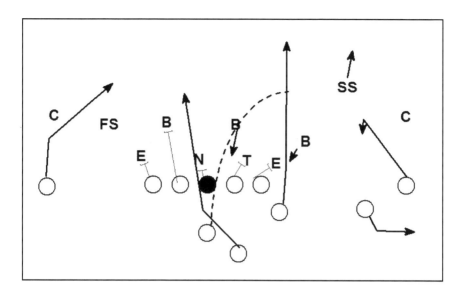

Diagram 28

We see many teams playing split safety looks because of the proliferation of spread offenses and trying to create an opportunity to try to confuse us on the offensive side the ball, and make it look different, you're getting lots and lots of defenses now that are leaving a lot of the grass down the middle of the field. There's a lot of room between the safeties and the sniffer allows you to take advantage of that.

The POP Pass plays nicely into our philosophy in the S2A, we tell our quarterbacks, anytime you get blitz, you are trying to punch the blitz in the mouth. If you can identify it pre-snap that it's coming, we want to throw the ball right where they're blitzing from. In this next image we are looking at a one high safety team (Diagram 29).

A one high safety defense won't have anybody to cover that zone except the free safety, so as long as the quarterback catches this, and gets it out of his hands quickly, there's nobody there to cover that. So if you're using the sniffer already, I would highly suggest you get the POP Pass taught. I think the most critical thing about the POP Pass is the footwork. If the tight end's first step is accurate, he's gonna have a good POP pass. If he doesn't have a good first step then you're gonna have a lot of issues right there.

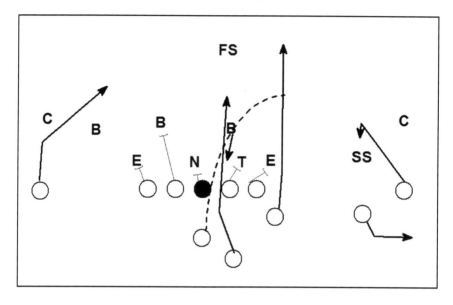

Diagram 29

On some of our POP Passes we are going to pair it with a veer cut inside zone look. What we're doing here is we're diving the back into the backside of the zone, so we're putting him basically right down into the lap of that five technique. We're running a POP Pass with the tight end, and we're running a spot concept with our outside two receivers we're doing it out of a compressed alignment (Diagram 30).

We run so much bubble stuff that people get used to jumping that, and there's lots of routes behind it. If the linebacker bails into the POP Pass, that's a give all the way by the quarterback, and we get a nice little four, five, six yard handoff right there.

So another thing you have to consider when you're installing all these POP Passes is, do you want to teach them as a lock RPO only? Or do you want to teach them locked, and unlocked? My specific advice is you teach it as a locked RPO first, I think it's easier to read, I think it's easier to teach.

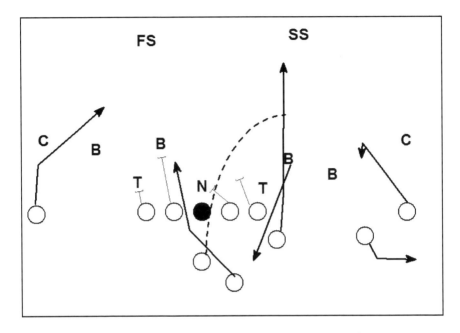

Diagram 30

But as you go along, you're going to want to unlock that RPO, and you're going to want to allow that quarterback to read the five technique in addition to keeping it locked because I think it gives you a multitude of answers. In this next image we will run an unlocked inside zone call with a POP Pass and a Bubble Screen attached to it (Diagram 31).

The R2 has to hang on the bubble up there. It leaves nobody in that zone right now to cover the tight end, so again there's a big chunk of grass right between the hash marks that you can throw to almost anytime you want. The Quarterback probably could go front door there if he really wanted to hold the ball but it's a safe pick is to just go ahead and play with the tight end. If the quarterback wanted to throw a pre snap out there to the two receiver side, he could've done that as well.

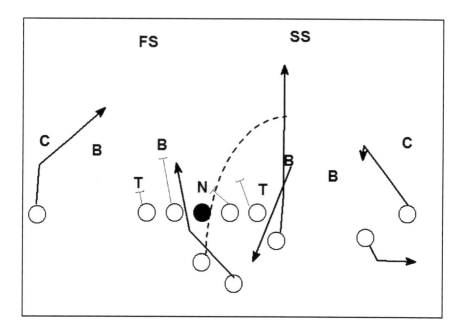

Diagram 31

Sniffer Flat Routes

There are many different ways to get the ball to the flat using a sniffer as well. Many times when we see an aggressive 3-4 defense we are going to lock them down. In other worlds we are going to block that five technique and read a linebacker. The Right Mike is going to trigger and be a box player the majority of the time. If he triggers, and he's a box player, and he's coming down then the quarterback automatically knows that we have three on two out here on the perimeter (Diagram 32).

We're not counting the R1, we're not counting that safety. So what we're actually running is a Snag Concept right there, and we're bringing the tight end as the flat guy and he runs that Arrow Route or Flat Route. As long as the quarterback sees the Mike staying in the box he knows he's going to have three on two down here to this strong side flat making it simply find the R2 and throw off of him. It really doesn't matter where that ball goes because you're three on

46

two, you're just gonna read that thing all the way out. It's a very, very simple way to get the ball to the flat.

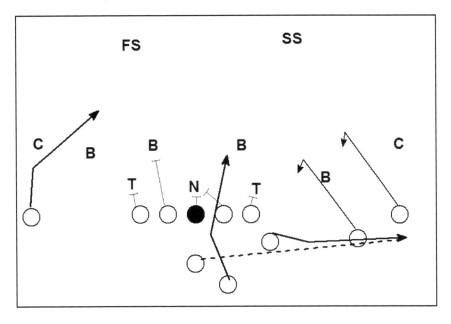

Diagram 32

Again, the defense is going to have a hard time playing man coverage to that because the only way they can play man coverage is they're going to have to have the Right Mike attached to that Flat Route. They don't want to do that because it leaves the box vulnerable. If we see that Right Mike running out of the box we're going veer cut inside zone and handing it to the running back in that open B gap.

Another easy way to get the ball to the flat is on a Bubble Route by the third receiver. When the sniffer is the third receiver he runs a Flat Route instead of a Bubble Route (Diagram 33).

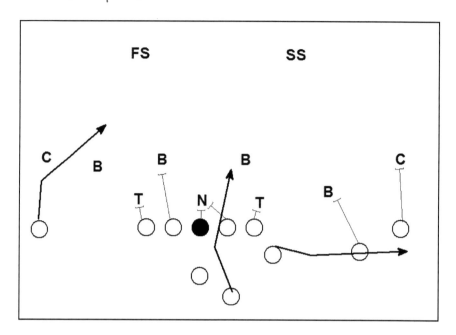

Diagram 33

If the Left Stack gets horizontal width, and we are locking it, we hand it off and run through the open B gap. So again, that's another way to really distort the defense. It doesn't always have to be with a POP Pass, sometimes the best way to distort the defense is to actually take that tight end horizontally to the flat. You can either execute a concept over there, or you can block it like we just did right there.

Split Zone

Split zone is something I really like. I think that you have to be very careful when you are self-scouting yourself to make sure that you split zone with the tight end on the same side of the formation he lines up on and the opposite direction and equal amount. Failure to do this will create a tendency for the defense to scout. I think if you don't have a steady balance of both of those two things the defense will really begin to get a tendency on you, and figure out wherever the sniffer is, the split is going to one side or the other.

So let's draw this up versus a 3-3 stack defense. We are going to show Bubble Screen oftentimes with the two receivers slit from the formation (Diagram 34).

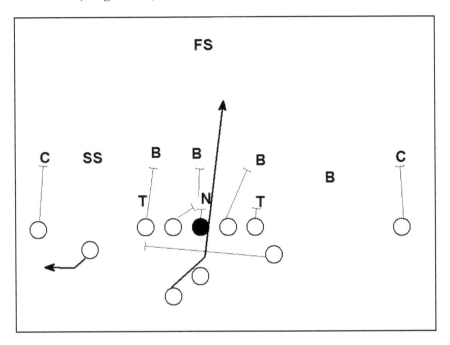

Diagram 34

We're showing them a balanced offense from a 2x2 set. They have to balance so many people up to defend grass, but there's only a limited number of blitz schemes they can bring. The defense, they're very cognizant of the fact that they can get out flanked, especially to the 2x2 sniffer side of the formation. This means that putting the sniffer to one side of the formation and then bringing him back to split zone on the two receiver side is tough on a stack team. Our default answer for the running back is anytime we have split zone, he's gonna push that ball to the front side, and if it's there he'll bang it, and take four yards. If he's unclear, he'll stick his foot in the ground, and he'll try to bend it and follow back to the sniffer. He'll try to bend it back, and as soon as he sees a crease, he'll hit it vertically. So in a very real sense, split zone, and a locked call are almost the same thing to us

49

from a back field alignment situation. The mechanics, the footwork, the aiming point in the back field on split zone, and on locked zone are almost the same and they have a lot of similarities in what you're trying to do with it.

Now let's draw up a 4-2-5 defense and assume they roll down into what they consider their eight man front or 4-4 look. When the sniffer splits the zone the back will push and then cut and there's a huge crease right there, and the running back gets a good head of steam up to the front door side, and then just slides and glides (Diagram 35).

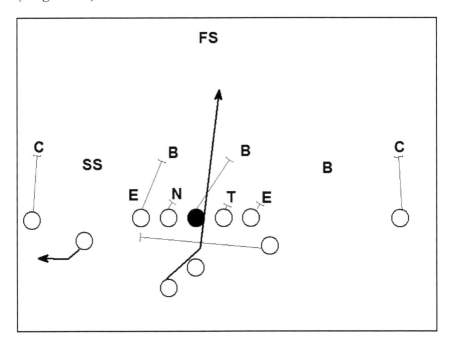

Diagram 35

The key coaching point there is as soon as he slides and glides, if he gets his shoulders square to line of scrimmage he needs to hit that a thousand miles an hour. We tell him, as soon as you've made the decision that you're gonna cut back to the sniffer you need to put your head down and you need to hit it right now and assume that there's going to be grass right there because if you slow play that in any way, and you don't hit it fast there will be a linebacker fill or you'll run into the back of an offensive lineman.

Counter Trey

We used to pull guard and tackle quite a bit back in 2011 and 2012. Lately, we didn't want to do that, we didn't have the athletes to do that, so now we started to get into a lot more GY Counter making our guard the trapper and our sniffer the wrapper. We can lock, or we can unlock that counter RPO. Now, sometimes defensive ends won't chase inside zone, but if you start pulling people, they will chase. And when you start sifting that right tackle to the second level, and you will see some hats start coming to the party. This will make defensive ends crash which gets your quarterback on the perimeter and now you can have a Bubble Screen with your two receivers and their R2 is stuck between two different players (Diagram 36).

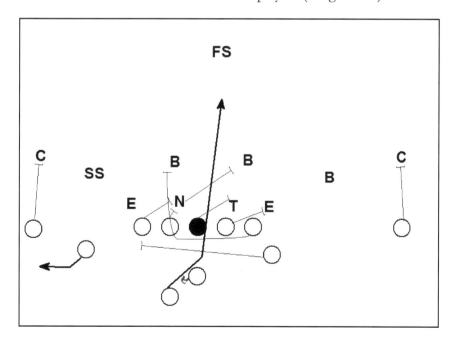

Diagram 36

To me, this is the epitome of triple option. So if you remember back to the five things we said at the beginning, in the sniffer set we want to change the surface, we want to provide an extra gap, we want to have split and load options, we want new ways to attack grass, and we want to isolate defenders to aid the triple option. Well, this is isolating defenders to aid the triple option. Their R2 has been hung out to dry by his base alignment. He's got six interior defenders who see double pull, and a tailback downhill, and they all want to go be a hero, and play dive. So it is likely that half the football team will be playing dive, and they're leaving that R2 out there on an island where he has a pitch back (Bubble Screen) and the quarterback. The R2 can't be right.

You can change the formation and use stacked receivers with the sniffer as well into the boundary. I love this because it creates a ton of grass up on the field side of the formation. So now you can now pull two guys back to the field, and have those big running lanes where you can hand off counter trey (Diagram 37).

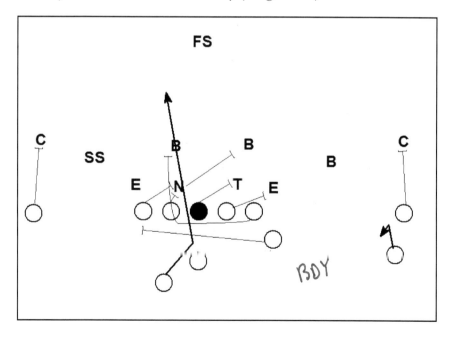

Diagram 37

So it's a great manipulation of the defense using the sniffer. That formation is a problem when you shove it all into the boundary because they cannot allow you to just hand that ball off and run outside zone into this boundary. And sometimes we'll even let the running back lead block and we'll run quarterback outside zone into the boundary if you don't respect this formation. The Sniffer forces the defense to play an extra gap outside, so that you don't just run outside zone, which gives you a ton of ability to pull that sniffer and go back the other direction. We are able to put the sniffer in the game and really screw with their assignment conflicts, add a lot of gaps, and make life difficult for them.

The next set is a 3x1 sniffer set to the field but with the tailback to that side it's basically a quads set. Now we are going to do is swing that back behind the X and the H receiver to the wide side of the field, pull the guard and sniffer back to the boundary, and let the quarterback read the defensive end (Diagram 38).

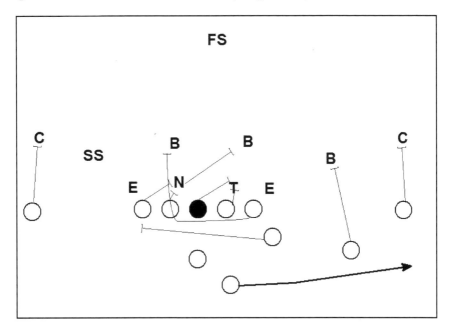

Diagram 38

53

If the defensive end goes with the back then the quarterback runs it. If the defensive end crashes on the quarterback then the quarterback throws it to the running back. There are tons of different things you can create with the sniffer and change the surface and structure of the defense. The sniffer makes it as difficult as possible for them to identify the offense, and makes the defense assign more gaps to the line of scrimmage. When you bring the sniffer into the game, you're hurting the defense because you're forcing them to assign guys to gaps, and when they're assigned to gaps they can't blitz, and they can't zone drop as easily. It really takes a lot of the options out of their defensive playbook, and it's making them play a lot more vanilla. Now having said all that, a gigantic asterisk I would like to put out there is I think some people have gone so far on this they're using the sniffer too much. I'm seeing some people that never get out of sniffer sets, that's all they play. I think it has a place, I think it has a huge place in the game of football right now, but it can't be overdone. There needs to be some common sense added to that.

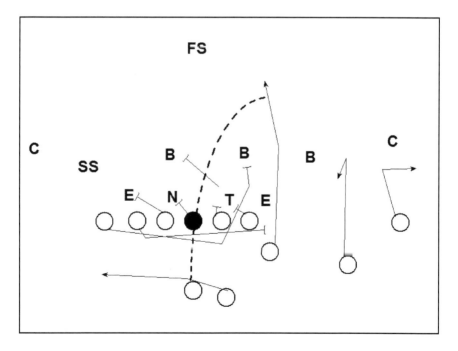

Diagram 39

Sometimes we run special versions of plays at the start of a contest. This is a special play we use at the start of the game, this is a quarterback split zone counter with a POP Pass added to it (Diagram 39).

Outside Zone

Outside zone to me is a critical component in why you want to get into a sniffer set. It is great to run versus a 3-3 stack team because they have a fundamental problem already. Their problem is they have three linebackers in the box who will have a lot of trouble getting outside the box. I can call Hitch Routes to the two receivers into the boundary and now it's just a matter of my tight end comboing up to their R2 defender and I can just basically run the ball into that giant area of grass to the field side (Diagram 40).

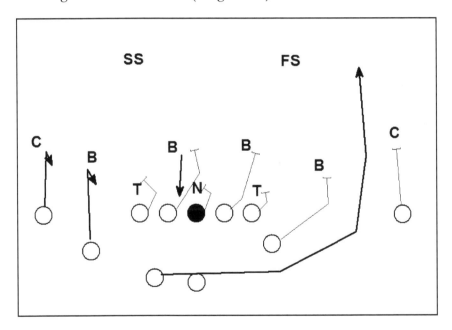

Diagram 40

By keeping twins into the boundary I'm able to hold a large number of people back into the boundary side, hand the ball off, and run into green grass. If the defense chooses to blitz from the inside they allows us to pick another guy off and make a big run. Outside zone has to be a major component of running the sniffer set. The defense has to respect the fact that you will hand the ball off that you will circle the field, and you will put the ball into the D or the E gaps. I think that's a really important piece in being successful with the sniffer is being willing to run outside zone. I see a lot of people that only want to run inside zone or they only want to insert the sniffer. I think all those things are great but you'll get a ton of extra real estate out of it after you've scared the defense with outside zone.

We tell our running back that his job is to circle the field. That means get outside and circle the field until the first wrong colored jersey crosses his face. When the first wrong colored jersey crosses his face, he is going to shoot north south immediately, put his toe in the ground, and run inside zone path. It's a great thing about outside zone, all those linemen are on a track, they're all working hard to reach and overtake. If you can't get reach and overtake, stick your foot in the ground, go north south, you're probably gonna find a crease.

Bucksweep

A great compliment to the outside zone play is Bucksweep. When we call Bucksweep we are going to block down with the sniffer, down with the tackle, and pull both guards. The great thing about the RPO situation is I don't need the running back for anything. So I'm actually having the running back lead out there on your L2 defender, and then I'm running a Now Screen to the outside receiver (Diagram 41).

The rules for the quarterback are actually quite simple, if you can circle the field and you've got clean grass out there just keep right on going. If it closes off, go ahead and pop it out there to the X receiver, and let him go get it. We're basically making the defense play an A, B, C, D, E, F, and almost a G gap all to the wide side of the field. And we've put them in a great deal of conflict.

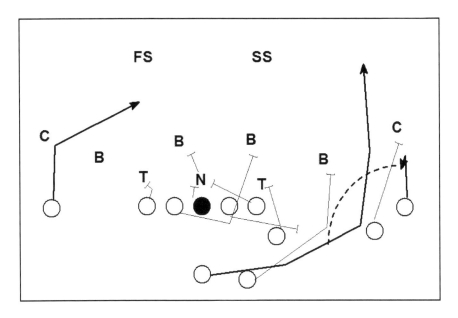

Diagram 41

I know everybody wants to call it pin and pull now, there's a lot of different ways to block it. To me it's still just Bucksweep. I love Bucksweep. I loved Bucksweep 20 years ago when I started out coaching in the Wing-T. The problem is Bucksweep is a more expensive play than outside zone, and I hear a lot of people contradict themselves on that, but people will say, "Well, buck is just down block and pull, it's really easy." Not if it's a shade over there to the sniffer set. It does become more complicated and not if the defense is slanting. Outside zone to me is everybody steps, and everybody runs a track, and easy to teach, and it's really consistent versus all fronts and stunts. I think if you've got the time try and run both plays.

Load Option and Front Door Throws

Load Option is defined as when the tight end is going around to block the outside linebacker. In this diagram we have a simple Now Screen on the back door side of the play and a Grass Concept to the front door side (Diagram 42).

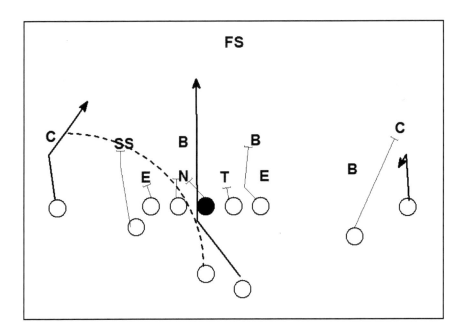

Diagram 42

I think one of the biggest advantages to all this extra gap stuff that you do with the tight end is you create lots of front door opportunities. The single side receiver is going to run a three step Slant Route but he might catch a 45 yard touchdown pass. Quarterbacks love this, receivers love this, there's huge opportunities to the front door side when you start inserting tight ends into the game. The defense has to be so gap conscious of this triple option back door side of the field that you create a lot of cheap and easy throws to the front door side. The Load Option outnumbers the defense and makes them more conscious of numbers and invites more one on one front door options.

I would say probably four or five of our longest touchdown passes this last year were throwing front door slants off of some sort of sniffer RPO on the back door side. The defense has to equate a ton of gaps to that Sniffer side, especially if it's a sniffer 3x1 side. There's so many things I can do, and there's so many defenders have to play that side honestly, that basically they run out of people, and when they run out of people they're going to rob the front door side to try to get an extra hat in the box, and when they do that there's a huge opportunity for you to throw front door grass especially against odd man front defenses (Diagram 43).

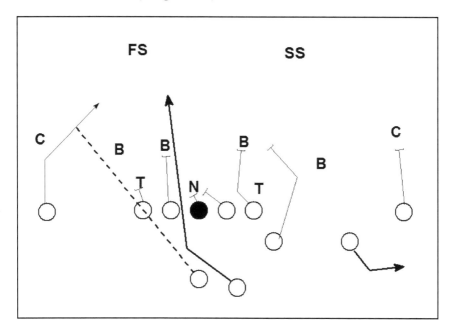

Diagram 43

So if you're having trouble getting the ball thrown to the front door side of your RPOs, putting a sniffer on the back door side is a great way to go about that. When we take another look at another diagram here of inside zone with a front door throw. Here we have another inside zone with a POP Pass. We're supposed to have a slant to the front door receiver, and our quarterback changes it to a Fade Route (Diagram 44).

If you're gonna play inside leverage to our front door side, you're gonna get this, and you're gonna get it more than once. We're going to go ahead and tee that thing up and we're going to throw the fade ball.

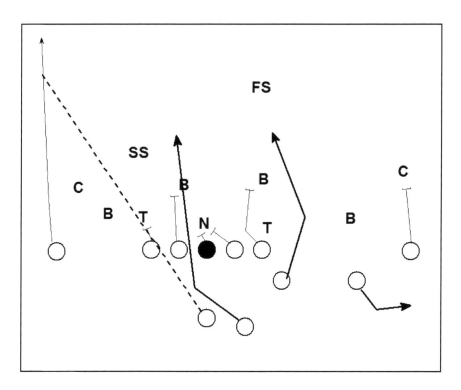

Diagram 44

The quarterback is conditioned to understand that if he has the option and the opportunity to throw touchdowns on the front door side, he doesn't have to ask my permission. He's got carte blanche to go throw those touchdowns whenever he wants. He's got inside press with no safety help then he can ask that receiver to run a Slant or Fade Route and take a 40 yard touchdown. That's just a natural progression and a natural thing we're going to allow our quarterbacks to do is have that freedom.

Split Zone

So in this next diagram we have sniffer 3x1 to the field side and we can make the defense shift people over there. So we're going to run split zone and control all six gaps so they can't get pressure and throw a single side receiver Hitch Route (Diagram 45).

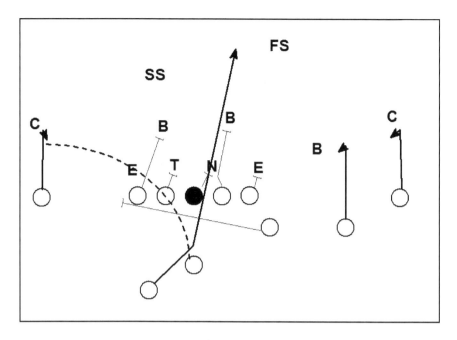

Diagram 45

This is a great way to get the ball to the perimeter on a defense is you're using this formation because they are influenced to think field side and you throw to that single receiver side. That's a great way to matriculate the ball down the field, and move people around using a variety of techniques inside the Surface To Air System.

Let's look at split zone versus a 4-2-5 defense. If the defense has already given up a throw to the single receiver side, they may push an extra hat out over there. That means the H receiver in the slot will be basically uncovered (Diagram 46).

That's a huge problem you will see with 4-2-5 defenses. They have to decide, do they want to take away the grass to the single side, and prevent that slant from going to the house? Or do they want to pull that rope back down to the two receiver side? That formation 2x2 with a sniffer tied in is a huge problem for 4-2-5 defenses, and to me it's a go to answer to utilize on them if that's what they're gonna try to come out and play. You're really making them decide what to do with that R2 player. Does he play the grass side or the opposite side? That's a huge, huge problem.

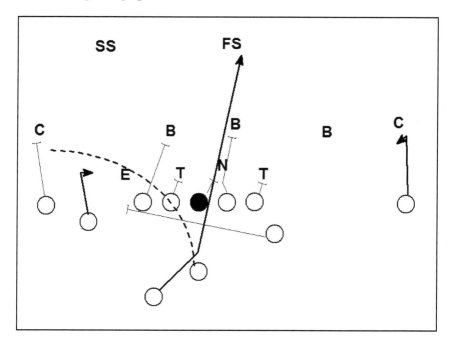

Diagram 46

Formational Variations

Here we are looking at a 3x1 set with a stack formation. So what you've basically done to the defense now is they have to make sure that you don't insert the tight end, so the Left Mike has to play the B gap. They're playing a wide five technique because they don't want to get out flanked, but their L2 knows there's going to be two guys that can potentially reach that defensive end. So that means he has to cheat and apex halfway between the stack receivers and the sniffer (Diagram 47).

That formation has naturally put them in a bad situation because now we can throw the ball to the stack receiver and let him run what amounts to an iso but 20 yards from the ball for a 10 plus yard game most likely. We have taken the sniffer and created a formation around him that has created a lot of dissension for the defense and put them in quite a bind.

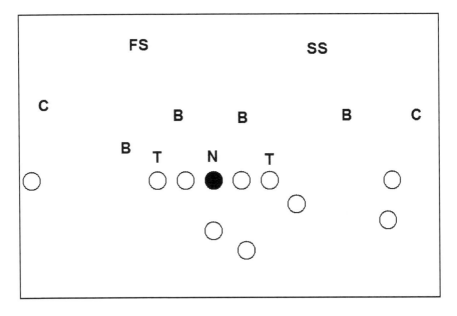

Diagram 47

Now let's take a look a 3x1 sniffer set but with the receivers out on the numbers. So now the defense has to decide how to handle the sniffer (Diagram 48).

We know we can POP Pass, we know we can kick out, we know we can load option, we know we can insert. The defense has to have all these people covering the tight end because we've done a good job getting him the ball throughout the year. Their L1 has to come all the way downhill and make the tackle on the Bubble Screen. He might do so but he's not going to do so before we get our five, six, seven yards. The Sniffer is causing them to have to add people to the box to play gaps, and not get out flanked, and not let us insert, and not let us POP Pass. And so that creates quite a few problems for the defense.

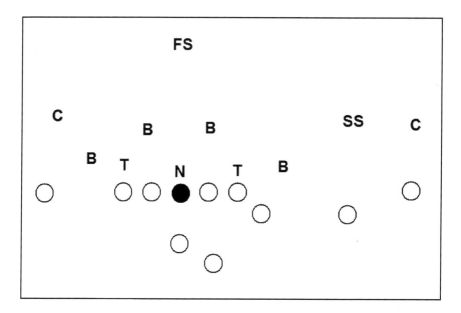

Diagram 48

Conclusion

The big thing I want to re-emphasize, to me there are five major reasons why you would want to use a sniffer. Number one it changes the surface of the defense. Number two it provides an extra gap to both the front door, and the back door side if you're doing it accurately. Number three it allows you to split, and load option the defense. Number four it allows you to find new ways to attack the grass that's already there. And number five, it isolates defenders, and it aids in the triple option, which is really what the RPO based offense is.

So again, I think if you're trying to manipulate defenses, a steady dose of sniffer is a really big, and really critical part of that. In the Surface to Air System we always say, everything we do has to be executed out of a 2x2, 3x1, 3x2, and sniffer alignment. If it cannot be run out all those things, then it's simply not a part of our package. And as the years have progressed, the sniffer has become a bigger, and bigger part of what we do, but I think a really key point of emphasis here is, the sniffer should be a big part of what you do, but it should not become your whole offense. There is still a place for 2x2, 3x1, 3x2, and all those things need to be a symbiotic relationship with the sniffer, and I think that's really, really important.

4
QSO

In this chapter we are taking a look at our quick/slow option style of football that we call a QSO. This is defined as a quick pass or screen paired with a slow screen on the same play. We ran this play all the way back in 2016 and at that time we called it Monarch. In this first diagram we are aligned in a 3x1 set to the field. We are going to run the Spot Concept to the field and then we're running monarch back to the boundary (Diagram 49).

The left tackle and left guard block solid. They block quick game. We then assign the right tackle, right guard and center to leave on the tunnel. This worked for us to an extent, but I'll show you here in just a minute why we changed some things. Monarch was our QSO back then, you can see our running back is supposed to have the corner. We get a couple linemen out there in front, they just create kind of some screen doors out there for the receiver and provide him some room to run. I have an almost pathological desire to stay away from 3rd down and Long, I really prefer to stay away from 3rd down period. I think this entire concept is for us to use on 2nd down and long, maybe even 2nd down and Medium. It is definitely good when you get into 3rd down situations.

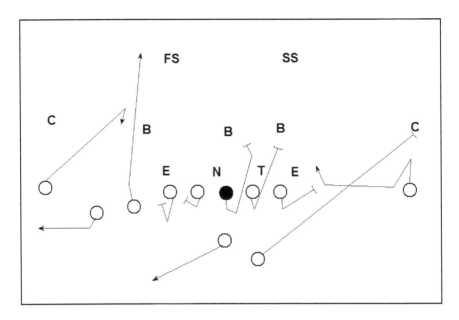

Diagram 49

As you build these QSOs all the quick games concepts are eligible for you, so any kind of quick concepts you want to utilize will work. For the purpose of this chapter we will stick with a basic Snag Concept for the sake of simplicity but any Surface To Air System quick concepts can be paired with the slow screen. What we are really trying to accomplish is to get rid of our traditional slow screens and replaced them with QSO stuff. We threw tunnel really well in 2017, but we only threw it to one kid and we only threw it in one direction. We were bad at slip screen.

Two years ago, we were great at slip screen. We were terrible at tunnel. The problem is, I hate practicing them because there's always a time where you've got to stop and you've got to say "Okay, it's Slow Screen time." Usually we would teach slow screens during blitz period. The defense knows it's coming, they're pinning their ears back. Then they realize it's Screen period, they stop, they blow it up, they create all kinds of problems, the quarterback doesn't get an accurate read. So over the last couple of years, we've tried to start going back and adding piece by piece outlet throws for the quarterback. I'm going to show you how easy this is to read and it's like everything else we do in the Surface To Air System. You've got to make the quarterback understand conceptually what he's really about and what he's trying to do in each of these concepts. So I'm going to make it really simple for you. I'm going to give you a couple of quick points such as on tunnel screen the ball is going to the outside receiver.

Let's take a look at a 2x2 call with a Snag Concept attached to the QSO (Diagram 50).

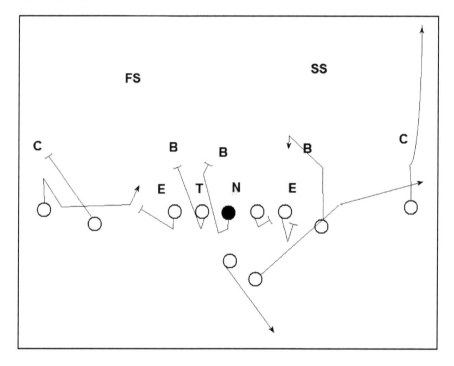

Diagram 50

If you are the back side, you are blocking solid. If you're the right tackle, you're going to block the defense end. That's it, block him. I don't care where he's at, I don't care where he goes. Block him. If you are the right guard, you're going to block the first down lineman that you can block. So if that's a three technique, a two, a shade, a nose, I don't care. He's yours. The backside tackle is going to kick slide to the inside, open up his hips and pray to god we get an outside rush. If we get any kind of outside rush, we're going to attach and run him right past the quarterback for all he's worth. If we get an inside charge, we're going to step back down. We're going to post step it back down after our kick slide and we're going to drive block him and try to drive him vertically because he's the one that's going to cause a problem.

The other two guys, the guard and center were both going to kick set that thing inside just a little bit. We're going to bring hat high and we're going to punch once. So we're going to get our hands on something. As soon as our hands make an attachment, we're going to leave. The H receiver is going to kick out the L3, the guard is most likely going to kick out L2, and the center is going to run the same path as the left guard until he gets a peel back. He's going to peel back on the first threat he sees. We're going to tell the X receiver to foot fire up, retrace his steps, and try and come back and try to catch that ball in that tunnel lane basically just outside of where the defensive end lines up.

Now let's look at how we read these sort of plays. There is a basic coach speak way to read this such as count the numbers of receivers to the quick game side and you read that defender from the sideline. Now, I would not talk to my quarterback that way so let me tell you how I talk to my quarterback. I would say, "Who is the third guy from the sideline in, not counting the safeties?" His answer better be the Mike Linebacker.

If the Mike leaves to the quick game side, you're throwing the screen every time. That's it, that's your job. If the Mike does not leave to cover the quick game, you're going to throw quick game. Now your read would be obviously on the R2. You'd throw it just like you'd throw any Snag Concept. The footwork is really important for the quarterback. I tell the quarterbacks to drop step your right foot, cross over plant, shuffle away, and lose ground to about seven yards deep.

When you get to the B gap, if you can throw the quick game based on the read, throw it. Play it, be done with it. If your read is pulling with you, stop and go into distress. Distress means start losing ground back behind that B gap and then throw the screen. If everything is covered, you should side arm the ball and one step hop it to the screen receiver.

So if everything gets blown up, they tackle the screen man, they cover all three of the receivers just one hop skip it to the X receiver. So that's a very simple look, we'd be reading the Mike and it's to a two man surface. Now, I'm counting the running back so I'm telling the quarterback right there, you have three eligible receivers so you find the defender commensurate with the numbers of receivers in the route. The third man from the sideline not counting the safety, that's the Mike.

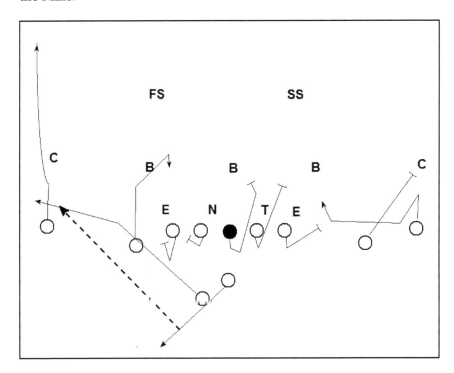

Diagram 51

In this next diagram we are 2x2 and we're throwing the Snag Concept to the right, and we're throwing screen to the outside receiver up top (Diagram 51).

So it's going to be to the outside receiver running the screen and the inside receiver is going to kick out the corner. We want the quarterback to lose ground to the B gap so then he is going into distress if he throws the screen he's got room to not get killed. In this instance, I think we could go ahead and throw the Snag Concept. You got two guys over there, if the Mike is not relating to it, go ahead and throw it out there and take what you can get. It does not matter which Surface To Air System concept you install right there, as long as you run it with the running back attached to it then it's a five man out concept and you're good. You've basically got two places to dump that football. You've got a running back in this right flat and you've got the X receiver up there to the left flat.

On a QSO if the defense wants to pin their ears back and bring a ton of a pressure, that's a key coaching point for the offensive line. Don't block, you should never block a second level defender on a slow screen. If you've got a guy that pins his ears back and he wants to run to the quarterback, let him pin his ears back and run to the quarterback. That's just fine. Don't hit a second level offender that's blitzing. When we practice QSO with our GPS, this is walks and then I'd take it out on the field. To me, a screen is eleven man concept of execution. You cannot do it with just skill players in my opinion because you've got to set up the box.

Now, I want to show you what we mean by distress. The quarterback loses that ground into the B gap and once he knows he cannot throw the Snag Concept, you can see what we mean by distress in this diagram (Diagram 4-4).

Distress means start losing ground. I call it letting the defense see blood in the water. Right now, the quarterback looks like he can throw the ball but when he goes into distress right there and loses those extra three or four yards, all those defensive players look at that and they say, "Here I come". It's like chum in the water, they're coming to kill it. If they've tagged it and they've decided to come after him, there's a pretty good chance when they see him go into distress if he's a good enough actor, that's a great place to go dump the football. Again, we're only getting two guys out, we're just getting the left guard and the center out in this.

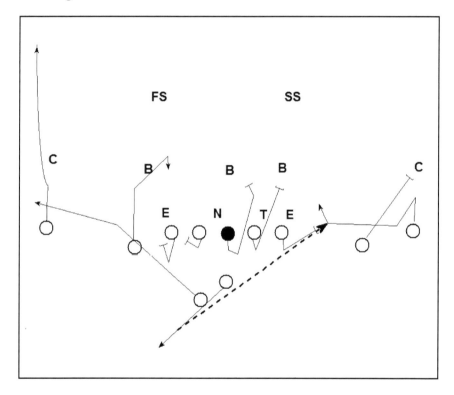

Diagram 52

If you want to experiment with it, if you want to try to get three guys out, be my guest. We've sometimes taken the tackle and as you saw in the film in 2016, we got him out. The reason I don't like it is there's a lot of big defensive ends that will bat that ball. That's the guy that will pick you off is the defensive end. I don't feel like the back side guard is ever going to get there anyway. So a lot of the times it's easier to just let him cut or just stay. So that's a pretty good look at tunnel to the outside receiver from 2x2.

In this next image we will look at three man snag now so we are in 3x1 right with a Snag Concept to the field and tunnel to the boundary (Diagram 53).

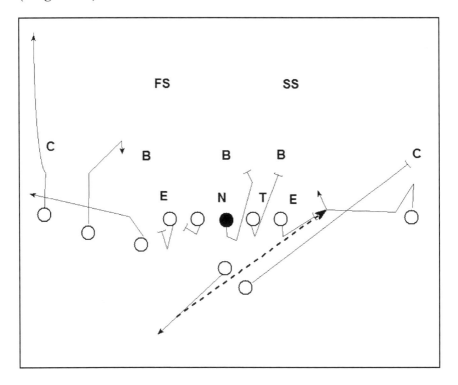

Diagram 53

The rules are all the same, nothing changes. The tailback is now the kick out guy.

It looks like a long run, the beauty of this is if they've got the L2 half influence apexed out there trying to be bit of a box player, as soon as he sees the tailback trigger and run for the flat, he would immediately assume there's either a screen out there or there's a wheel route out there.

Either tailback situation in his mind should get L2 to open his hip. If he's not already a blitz guy and a lot of times if he is a blitz guy, this will make him peel off that blitz and attach to the running back. So a lot of times when you run it this way, you'll get the L2 chasing the running back all the way out there before he realizes what it is and it sets up a great kill shot by your left guard to go ahead and kick him out and run right by the hole. I would tell that running back to cheat up and cheat out as far as he needs to make that thing happen.

I don't care if he knows if it's happening, sometimes if you get a really wide nine technique release, that tail back will have to go underneath there to get there. The key point is cheat him out, cheat him up and let him get out of that back field so he can go and make that kick out block. You've got to remember, the quarterback is being told by the time you hit that third step, that third shuffle step, it needs to come out. If you're going to throw the quick game, it's got to come out right now.

Now let's draw up the quick game concept to the single receiver side with a 3x1 set to the back side for the QSO (Diagram 54).

If we remember back to what the read rule was, there's two receivers. So now I'm really reading the second defender from outside in not counting the safety because the tailback is the second receiver. So now I'm reading R2. If R2 gets on his horse and chases that running back all the way to the perimeter, stick your foot in the ground, go into stress and throw the screen back.

If R2 allows himself to get outflanked, throw the ball on the quick game side because you're going to win over there. Essentially you've really got a double team on their L2 defender alright? The H receiver is probably going to identify him as the second man from the sideline and block him, and the guard is probably going to identify him as the same guy and he is going to be put in a vice and drive blocked out of there. The quarterback either hits the flat before they get there or he identifies it as a rush and he throws the screen. Either way, you're going to win.

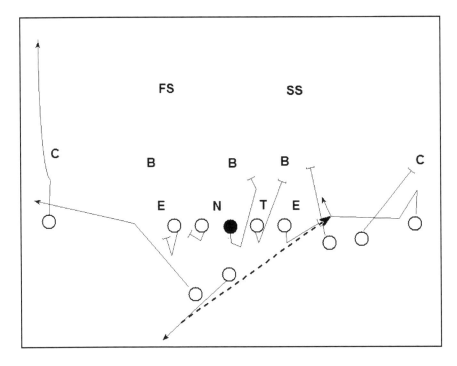

Diagram 54

Now we are drawing up a slip screen from a 3x1 set. I tell the X receiver if you know 100% it's man coverage and you can run outside the L3 and you can run into the end zone, run into the end zone. If you are 99.9% sure it's man coverage, then you've got to block it. The only way you can truly run him off is if you know he'll go with you. If you don't know, you've got to break down and stock it. Everybody's else's rules are the same except now because it's slip screen, the screen is going to the second receiver so that is the tailback here. The tailback is going to go through the B gap, kind of give a little shuffle step like he's setting up the pass pro, and then he'll leak and run that NFL style slip screen back into the flat (Diagram 55).

I think this is a great play to really bust the defense wide open if you're getting weak blitz. Anybody that wants to run corner blitz, L2 blitz, they want to try to get some kind of trap coverage stunt off of that short side of the field, this should be an immediate go to call.

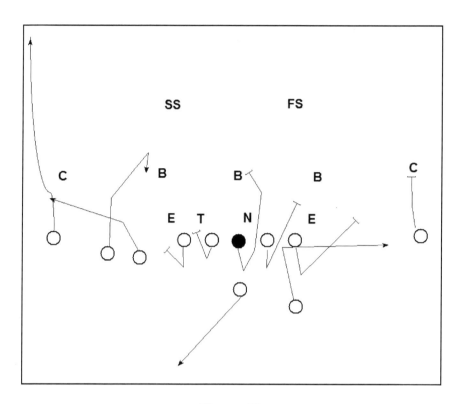

Diagram 55

If the tailback cannot get through the B gap, then he is told to go around the tackle. I don't care what you do, but you get your butt out there so the quarterback's got somewhere to go with that ball. We tell the tailback that we prefer you go through the B gap, but if you can't get through the B gap, oh well. The point is just get back into that flat and go.

So now let's draw up slip screen here into a 2x2 set surface (Diagram 56).

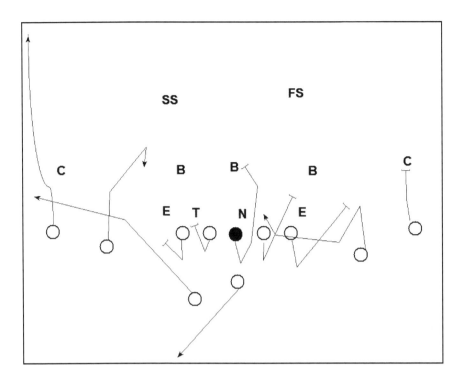

Diagram 56

We still have got the Snag Concept to the right, but now the H receiver should do that foot fire and he should come right back underneath the screening offensive lineman. He should drive up just enough to back his guy off and set the block up and then retrace his steps and get himself right back into the honey hole.

So now let's look at slip screen back to a three man surface. You're just going to tell that number two receiver to retrace your steps and catch it back at the line of scrimmage (Diagram 57).

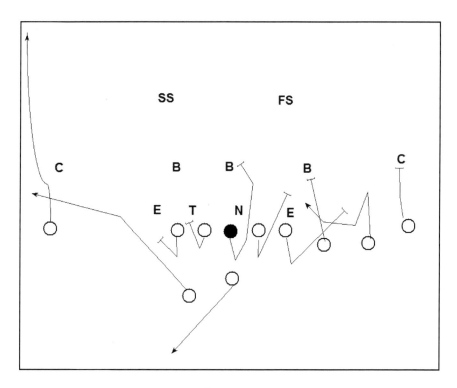

Diagram 57

The number two receiver is now able to work back underneath the offensive lineman in turn this into a middle screen. The ability to morph and move these formations around makes life hard on the defense.

Conclusion

The ability to play high percentage football on both 2nd and 3rd Downs is a key component in playing quality football in the Surface To Air System. The QSO package allows the offense to spread the ball around to all its eligible receivers and attack the grass all across the surface of the defense. The offense can line up with one, two, or three receivers to either the quick game concept side of the formation or the slow screen side of the formation. This ability to distort the formation and thereby change the number of receivers running quick passes or slow screens is a complicated world for the defense to process. These plays allow the offense to block almost no one in the box and invites the defense to bring rushers into the backfield that are then absorbed and taken away from the ball. Many times the offense can simply get in the way of defenders and have a fairly successful play.

These sorts of plays confound and frustrate the defense and keeps them from being confident in their pressure schemes. If the defense elects to stay back and not pressure then the quick passes are likely to eat up large chunks of real estate as well. These are full field RPOs that allow the offense to decide when and where the defense will be punished for attacking. These are yet another arrow in the shiver of a Surface To Air System play caller that can complicate the defensive structure and package and aid in offensive production.

5

LOCKED POP

A large number of people feel that POP Passes should be unlocked affairs. Other coaches feel that locked runs are the way to go for a POP Pass. Let's analyze first that a locked play is one where the defensive end on the back door side is blocked and an unlocked play is when the back door defensive end is unblocked. We are assuming that the offense is playing with a sniffer tight end on the back door side quite a bit on these type of plays. It is critical to discuss how to handle and block these sort of plays because the sniffer POP Pass has become a centerpiece of many RPO based offense in the game of football today.

Almost exclusively, we used to teach everything unlocked first. However, when we teach sniffer POP Pass we always teach it as a locked RPO first. You can leave it unlocked, the problem is you would almost have to throw the POP as the pre-snap and then read everything else around it all the way as a triple phase RPO. However, if you lock it, you can not only throw it as a pre-snap look, you can read the linebacker in the B gap for the post-snap and make this a pre-snap or post-snap RPO. The idea of teaching the POP Pass as a locked RPO allows the quarterback a great degree of flexibility and it is also quite easier to teach. The quarterback is able to manipulate defenders with his pre-snap look but he can also move the linebacker with his post-snap read.

So in this first diagram let's look at the POP Pass as a post-snap RPO with the offensive lineman executing a locked inside zone play (Diagram 58).

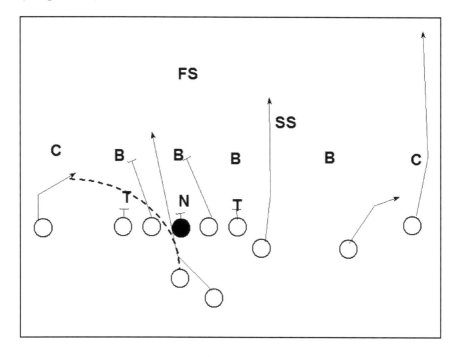

Diagram 58

If the linebacker attaches and takes the POP Pass away, then the quarterback should just hand the ball off. When the linebacker moves to open his hips in relation to the POP Pass then he is leaving the back door B gap wide open. The tailback is told to veer cut the ball into the back door B gap whenever there is a lock call for the offensive lineman.

This downhill posture by the tailback adds to the difficulty of the linebacker as the tailback's path and the sniffer's POP Pass basically leave him caught between two insertion points of the football. The only thing the quarterback is doing is reading that second level defender and basically making him wrong. If he's sitting there staring at the quarterback then he will ride the tailback on the mesh point and then throw the POP Pass.

In this next diagram we see the linebacker turning his hips and he's relating to the POP Pass which means he is in no position to fill the B gap. If the linebacker cannot fill that gap then the ball should be handed to the tailback and he will have extra space to hit the gap with the linebacker widening and retreating towards the POP Pass (Diagram 59).

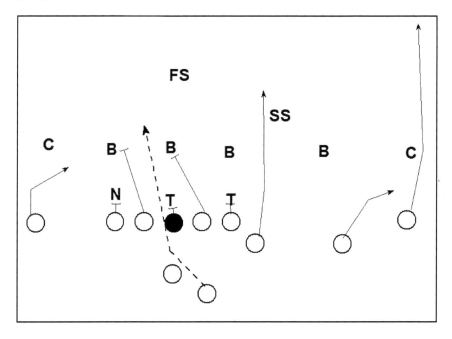

Diagram 59

The quarterback can also mesh and read this POP Pass with the POP pass not be a sniffer but an unattached receiver in a 3x1 set (Diagram 5-3).

So this diagram features an unattached receiver. The read is the same and we're reading that B gap defender still despite this new formation. The read is still if he comes down into the B gap, throw the POP Pass and if he rotates to the POP Pass the we will hand the ball off.

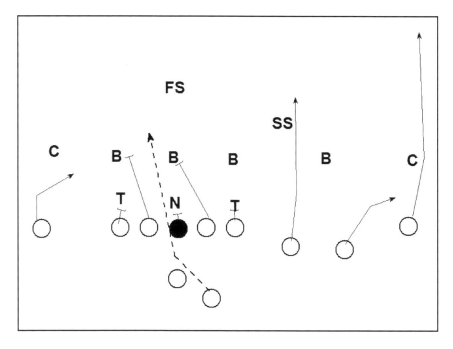

Diagram 60

The problem with 3-3 stack teams is it's hard to throw the POP Pass against them if the POP Pass receiver is coming from a sniffer alignment. When the POP Pass receiver is unattached and out in space he is harder for their Left Stack player to determine where to go. This player has to declare the box or the POP Pass to be his assignment and he has to move to it very quickly. This prevents the defender from really disguising his intentions and thereby speeding up the quarterback's read.

Conclusion

Teaching the POP Pass is an integral part of modern RPO based offenses. It is essential that an offense is able to feature this sort of play from both a locked and an unlocked structure. The offense is able to confuse the edge of the defense when they are capable of blocking the defensive end or locking the defensive end and reading the linebacker to that back door side. Teaching the POP Pass is critical but so is teaching the running back the correct path to insert into the back door B Gap.

Once these mechanical adjustments are made the quarterback's read is actually quite simple. It is common practice to put two receivers outside the sniffer and let them play some sort of two-man flat game against either the L2 or the R2 defender. As the quarterback gets better at reading the POP Pass from a locked RPO setting, the offense can progress to allowing this RPO to be unlocked as well. Most RPOs are taught from an unlocked setting and then worked back to a lock situation. However, in this sort of RPO is best to teach it as a locked structure first and then work backwards into an unlock setting.

Once the offense and the quarterback become proficient at reading this sort of play it can then be progressed to a motion-based RPO or an unattached third receiver running the POP Pass. There is a wide variety of window dressing that can be added to this type of RPO once the quarterback learns to read it effectively. Once again, it is a strong suggestion for the play caller today that you teach this sort of RPO locked first. This is a departure from what most RPOs are taught as but it is a great way to enhance and speed up the quarterback read progression and make this a viable and lethal part of your RPO based offenses.

6
3X2 RPOS

3x2 RPOs are a great way to attack modern defenses in the game of football today. Part of the reason this is true is that 3x2 sets help the offense to get the defense out of their basic defensive structure. The nature of a 3x2 set is that forces the defense to reduce its playbook options and limits its fonts, stunts, and coverage permutations. There are some nuanced changes that must be analyzed and explained about how this sort of RPO is executed. While these changes are unique and specific they are not difficult to understand as long as there's a clear cut and concise way to teach them. This chapter attempts to simplify the structure of a 3x2 set and the quarterback reads inside them.

We love to run gap scheme runs from 3x2 sets because we think that they are much more effective in creating angles against the defense. In this first diagram we are running a 1 Back Power Play (Diagram 61).

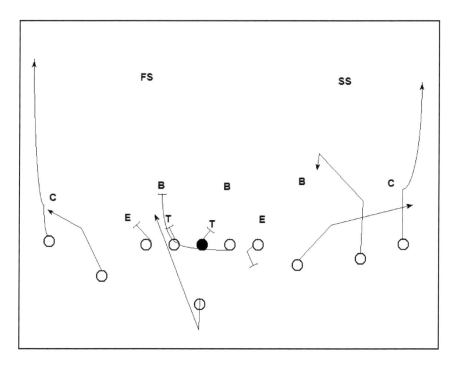

Diagram 61

We are pulling the left guard and we're pulling him up right through the right B gap. We're 1 Back Power to the right, and we are executing a Fade Flat Concept to the left, and a Snag Concept to the right. Now, just imagine for a minute I'm in one back. If I am in one back and the running back is running 1 back Power to the right then the right side receivers are the front door side of the concept. The left side is the back door because whichever direction the running back is going is the front door side. Now, when you run an empty RPO, it's backwards. And that's another thing that's always been in my head but not something that I ever really explained to any members until very recently. If the quarterback takes the snap, then the quarterback has to read the left side as his pre-snap side. Because his body is taking him to the right, the only thing that he can throw post-snap is the right side.

Try it yourself, take a snap and try to run to your right and throw the ball back to your left. It's not going to mechanically work. So this is what you have to tell your quarterback, just don't tell anybody else on the offense because they honestly don't need to know. I always think about people are on a need to know basis and they don't need to know. Tell the quarterback when you run an empty RPO, whichever side you're running towards is your back door side. If you're running 1 Back Power right, you tell your quarterback, "Look to your left side for your pre-snap side". If you've got pre-snap, throw it over there. If you don't, start running to the right and if that third defender comes to play in the box, throw the Snag Concept on the run. It's as simple as just slow down, raise up, and throw the pass play on the run.

Of course, if the linebacker does not relate to the box, follow the guard, run the power play. So tell your quarterback when you're running the ball in an empty RPO, the side you're running to is your post-snap read. That is your back door side.

There's a lot of people that say, "Well, you shouldn't run empty RPOs. The quarterback's in jeopardy..." I've heard that way too many times. I don't agree with any of that. I think empty RPOs are the simplest thing you can do because there's no mesh point, you're not asking the quarterback to stick it in the running back's belly and then pull it back out and throw. I think the younger and less experienced your quarterback is with RPOs, the more empty RPOs you should be running. It's cleaner pictures, it's easier reads, the defense can disguise less, he doesn't have to worry about a mesh point. It's just a heck of a lot simpler football to play RPO in empty than it is anything else. The quarterback can give a little jab step like he's going to run it downhill and then fire it back out there for the screen (Diagram 6-2).

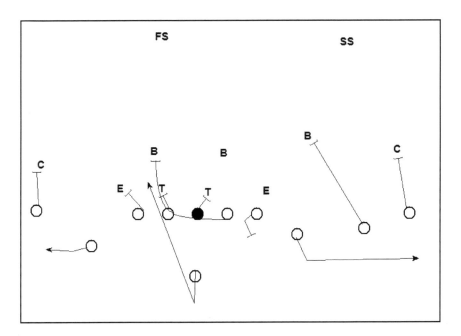

Diagram 62

The quarterback can be taught to give them a little fake trying to drag the defense down into the box with him and then kick it back out there and let some bad things happen to them.

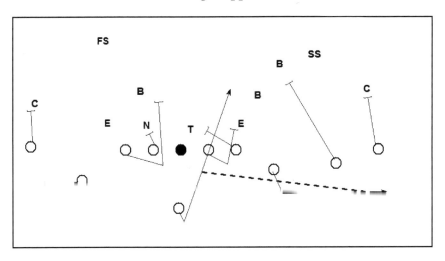

Diagram 63

88

In this next diagram we're running double fold to create some extra angles on the defense (Diagram 63).

The quarterback can run the ball left or he can post-snap it left. If he doesn't have three over three defenders, and there's only two over three he can kick the ball outside. That's the quarterback's post-snap side out there because the run is left, the post-snap is left. He can just kick the ball out, which outflanks the defense and let's that kid take off.

The next diagram is an inside zone lock call set to the right (Diagram 64).

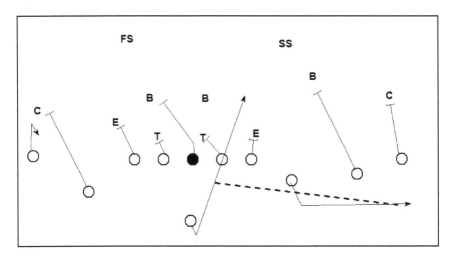

Diagram 64

We've got Now 1 on one side and we've got Now 3 on the other side of the formation. The quarterback probably reads that one side as man coverage, man for man, so he's going to post-snap the right hand side. In a perfect world, he would have stepped down at the line of scrimmage.

We can also utilize an outside zone play with the quarterback to the right hand side of the formation (Diagram 65).

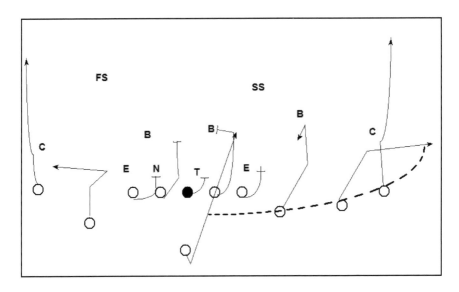

Diagram 65

The play is outside zone with a Stick Concept, so the quarterback could either run outside zone to the top or he could post-snap the stick up there.

We could also utilize quarterback draw with a Stick Concept to one side and a Slant Option Concept to the other side. As soon as that H receiver runs the Slant Option Concept and takes that defender with him, the quarterback's able to run that football. Now it's just one on one.

Another great empty RPO run concept is the tackle wrap. In this play our left tackle is wrapping for the dart play. We're running dart to the right so the post-snap side is to the right (Diagram 66).

You got three defenders covering two receivers. The third defender is kind of questionable whether he's in the box. The quarterback reads that as man coverage let's say, then he's going to run that all the way. If that defender is too close to the box then the quarterback would throw it. All these plays have the same cool idea in common which is that the quarterback can hold onto the ball until the last possible second and then make his decision once the defense commits to a course of action. This allows the offense to truly have the dry erase marker last.

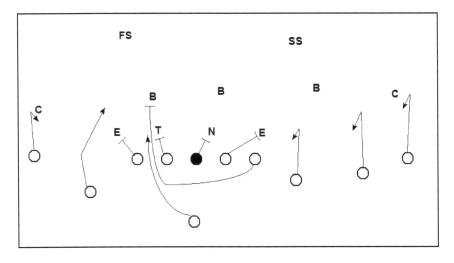

Diagram 66

Conclusion

I hear a lot of people talk about being concerned about their quarterback in 3x2 RPOs, I think the beauty of empty RPOs is you're baiting the defense to come out and bring pressure on you because if they bring pressure on 3x2 RPOs, there's a lot of really good things that are going to happen for you. I feel that the offense can force the defense to declare their intentions more easily from a 3x2 set than any other formation.

If you are a coach starting RPOs for the first time then I think 3x2 is an easy and safe way to go. Of course quarterbacks can be dinged up at any time and on any play, however, I feel that 3x2 RPOs allow them to attack the defense instead of standing back in the backfield and being attacked by the defense. The ability of the quarterback to hold the football and make his decisions at the last possible second on a pre-snap RPO means that he can delay his decisions a bit longer. This extra time allows the quarterback to make better and more informed decisions.

As you travel further into the RPO world then these sorts of RPOs can be window dressed and made to look more complicated but they remain one of simplest and most effective forms of moving the football in the game today.

7

STICK, SNAG, AND SPOT MOTION RPO CONCEPTS

The Stick, Snag, And Spot Concepts are a staple of the Surface To Air System because they all involve the same triangular read on the flat defender. All three of these plays feature deep route behind the corner, a flat breaking route, and some sort of route that attacks the outside linebacker.

These displays are so user friendly because they can be thrown as a quick game concept, a pre-snap RPO, or as a post-snap RPO. These plays have an amazing amount of versatility and they are critical components to the overall offensive attack. These are concepts that we install from our varsity team all the way down to our middle school feeder program and they are incredibly simple for our players to execute. Our quarterbacks find these plays very easy to read as well. While these plays are very simple to read and execute they are very versatile and can be tagged and mutated to disguise them from the defense and keep them useful and modern to our style of attack.

Stick Concept

The first concept we're looking at here is the Stick Concept. When we run the Stick Concept we're going to execute an outside release

Fade Route by the outside receiver. Our goal is we want to turn R3's hips and run him to the sideline. Obviously, if we get cloud coverage, trap coverage, where that R3 is coming down, the quarterback automatically throws that deep ball. If we get any kind of bail coverage out of the R3, then we're going to hit the flat runner. The player running the Flat Route will proceed up four steps and the speed cuts to the flat. The number three receiver, and in this first diagram he is in the backfield, is going to run a Hitch Route. He is going to hitch up right there where our number three receiver would be. Obviously, if we were in trips, and we put a third receiver out there, he'd just be running a standard Hitch Route (Diagram 7-1).

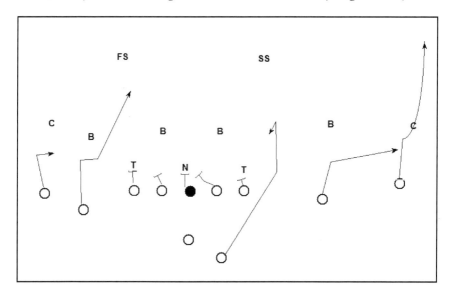

Diagram 67

For the quarterback, reading the Stick Concept is very simple. All these Stick, Snag, and Spot Concept calls are the same. If that corner, the R3 squats then we are throwing the deep ball. If that corner bails, we are simply reading the R2, in most cases the flat defender, and we're throwing off of his movement key. If we have a lot of issues with the Mike pushing out of the box, then you would obviously need to RPO this play to account for the Mike. So this is the basic pass play non-RPO concept for the Stick Concept. If we execute the

Stick Concept from a 3x1 set then the same routes are executed except for the fact that the third receiver is now the H receiver and he executes the Hitch Route (Diagram 68).

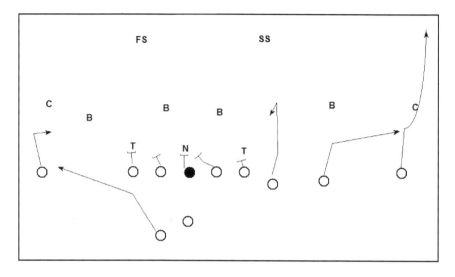

Diagram 68

The tailback is in the backfield and set away from the 3x1 set as a default rule in the Surface To Air System. For the purpose of this chapter the tailback is always set away from the 3x1 set on all non-RPO pass plays. As the tailback is set away from the 3x1 set he will check for a blitz and then execute a Flat Route if there is no threat to the quarterback from this side of the formation.

The Stick Concept can also easily be paired with an RPO style of reads. If the Stick Concept is an RPO read from a 2x2 set it involves a triple option read on the perimeter (Diagram 69).

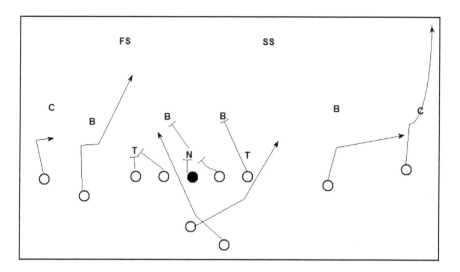

Diagram 69

The quarterback would read the Grass Concept and the Stick Concept as pre-snap throws. If he cannot make a completion based upon a pre-snap evaluation then he will progress to a post-snap read of the defenses. This read will be based upon a read on the defensive end. If the defensive end feathers then the quarterback would simply hand the football off. However, if the defensive end were too crash and take away the diving tailback then the quarterback would execute a pull and attack the R2 defender on the perimeter of the defenses.

If the R2 attacks the quarterback then he would throw the Flat Route to the Y receiver but if the R2 stays with the Y receiver the quarterback would just run the football. This play is a simple and articulate manifestation of the best aspects of the triple option offense. I have long maintained that RPOs are really just an evolving and modern day adaptation of that tried and true offensive attack system.

The 3x1 Stick Concept RPO is also an easy and consistent read for the quarterback (Diagram 70).

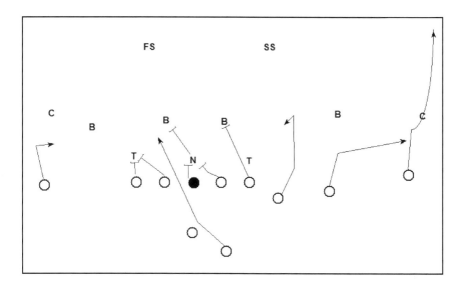

Diagram 70

This play can be thrown as a pre-snap or as a post-snap read for the quarterback. If the third receiver is uncovered then this will often result in a snap throw to the H receiver in space as he is often not covered on his inside leverage side of the play. If the defense chooses to take this route away then the quarterback can progress all the way to the post-snap phase of the RPO and read the play all the way out.

Snag Concept

The Snag Concept has long been a reliable mainstay of what we have tried to do in the Surface To Air System. The play is universally capable of being run versus man coverage or all the zone coverage families that we see in the game of football today. These route structures are incredibly durable and malleable as we will see in later sections of this chapter. The outside receiver must run an unconditional outside release Fade Route, This route serves the same purpose for the Snag Concept that it did for the Stick Concept which is that it turns the R3 player's hips and prevents him from putting his eyes in the backfield. If the R3 stays in the flat then the quarterback

97

must throw the Fade Route.

On all these concepts the quarterback must attack a defense that traps or keeps the R3 defender in the flats. This is true on all these plays and is the first read for the quarterback on Stick, Snag, and Spot Concepts. The second receiver pushes up three steps, two steps toward the slant, and then shuffles and sets his feet and posts up to the quarterback. The third and final receiver in the route structure runs a Flat Route attempting to expand and attack the R2 defender for width (Diagram 71).

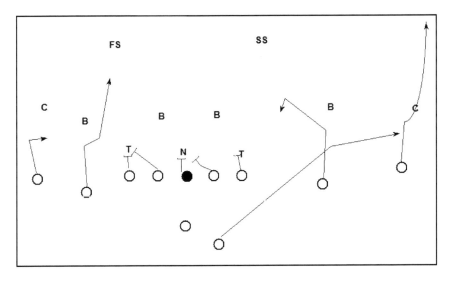

Diagram 71

This structure attacks man coverage because the Flat Route is likely to outrun the linebacker charged with covering him. If the R3 player bails in any zone coverage then the R2 defender is trapped between the Snag Route and the Flat Route and is an easy read for the quarterback.

The 3x1 structure of this play is very easy to read as well and while not as good against man coverage, because the tailback is not leaving the box to create deception, it is actually a great way to attack zone coverage families (Diagram 72).

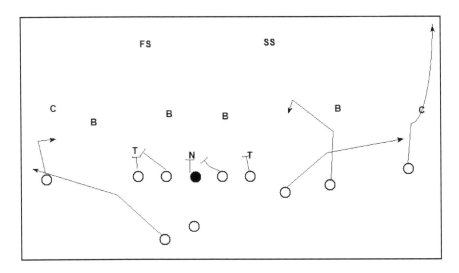

Diagram 72

The back side of the concept has a Slant Route and a Flat Route by the tailback. The quarterback has a very easy and very standard read versus all zone coverage families from a 3x1 set.

The Snag Concept is also a great way to build a 2x2 RPO concept. The advantage of the 2x2 Stick Route and 2x2 Snag Route are very similar except that the Snag Route actually provides a stationary platform for the quarterback to throw the ball in to instead of a moving target (Diagram 73).

The quarterback can throw the Snag Concept as a pre-snap throw or he can read the defensive end and progress to a post-snap read on the R2 defender after reading the defensive end.

At this point all of the RPOs we have looked at have been unlocked calls. This means that the defensive end is unblocked or unlocked. We teach all RPOs as an unlocked surface before we allow the quarterback to learn them from a locked structure. The definition of a locked RPO is one where the defensive end is blocked by the offensive tackle. When an RPO is locked the quarterback takes his read back one player to the linebacker directly behind the defensive end and is responsible for the B gap.

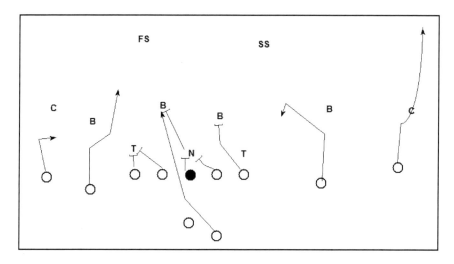

Diagram 73

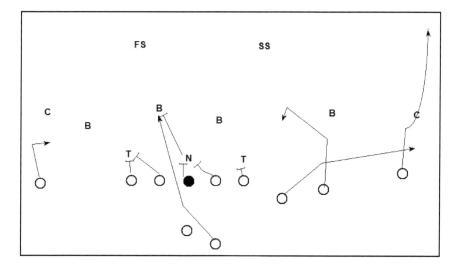

Diagram 74

The reason that a coach might elect to utilize a locked RPO is because it keeps the quarterback safer, and slow down his read so that he can have an easier time manipulating a second level defender over a first level defender. The Snag Concept from a 3x1 set is a great way to introduce your quarterback to a locked RPO (Diagram

7-8).

The quarterback is able to place his eyes on the Right Mike and just gauge where his movement will take the ball. If the Right Mike fills the gap then the ball will come out to the perimeter but if he works for width then the quarterback will hand the ball to the tailback working through the B gap. This is an easy and concise way to teach the quarterback to read locked RPOs from a 3x1 structure.

Spot Concept

The Spot Concept is a great passing concept that has taken on more significant the last few years as more and more teams have begun to use it. The second receiver runs a six step Corner Route and serves as the deep route runner for this concept. The outside receiver runs to a spot here the Snag Route would be run if the inside receiver were to be running it. The third receiver, in this first diagram the tailback, executes a Flat Route (Diagram 75).

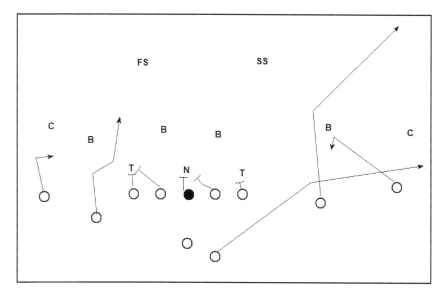

Diagram 75

The quarterback reads the play the exact same way he read the other plays we have mentioned in this chapter. If the R3 player bails then the read is on the R2. However, if the R3 stays low in the flat the quarterback must throw the Corner Route and punish the defense for attempting to keep the extra defender in the low flat area of the field. The 3x1 version of the flat simply adds the H receiver as the Flat route runner (Diagram 76).

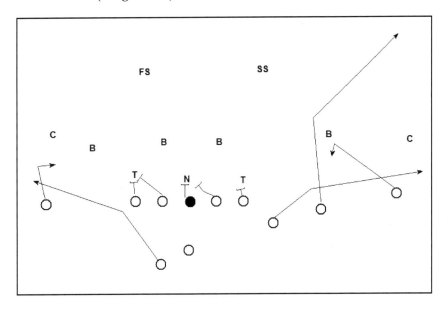

Diagram 76

The tailback once again works away from the 3x1 surface to hold the defense on the weak side and provide extra protection for the quarterback.

The 2x2 Spot Concept RPO is designed to be a highly effective post-snap RPO. This play is almost exclusively taught as an unlocked RPO where the defensive end is being read by the quarterback (Diagram 77).

If the defensive end crashes and takes away the dive by the tailback then the quarterback will pull the football and attack the R2 player very quickly. The R2 is very likely to attack the quarterback because he will assume the outside receiver has disappeared when the slot receiver progresses vertically.

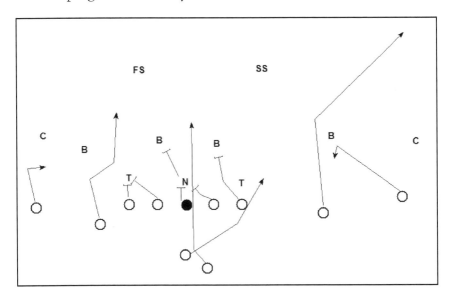

Diagram 77

Oftentimes, the R2 will attack the quarterback after his pull and the ball will be thrown behind the R2 to the Z receiver on the Spot Route. This is a highly effective post-snap RPO from this 2x2 alignment.

The 3x1 RPO version of the Spot Concept is another variation that is a great candidate for a locked RPO (Diagram 78).

Once again we will read the Right Mike and if he works for width into the flat then the quarterback will replace him by handing the ball to the tailback. If, however, the Right Mike stays in the box and plays the run then he will allow the defense to be outnumbered on the perimeter and the quarterback should pull the ball and throw it to the flat. The locked RPOs we utilize in the Surface To Air System such as this one are very user friendly and allow the quarterback to manipulate the second level defender very effectively.

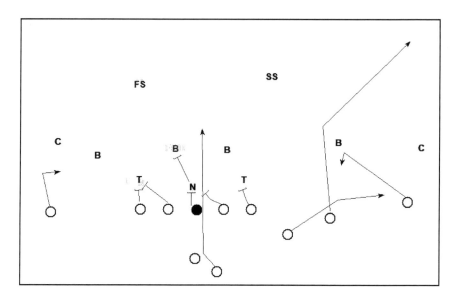

Diagram 78

Motion RPOs

The Surface To Air System features a large number of permutations in its RPO menu. These RPOs are all designed to attack specific parts of the defense and their tendencies and reactions to what we are attempting to accomplish. The Stick, Snag, and Spot Concepts are all huge parts of this RPO package. There is an intriguing aspect that can be added to our RPO package which is to incorporate motion into these plays.

The motioning of receivers changes the surface of the play structure and makes it much more difficult for the defense to process out what the RPO looks like and what the route structure is on a given play. For the purpose of simplicity, we will only diagram the Snag Concept in this section but articulate six different motions in the section that follows.

The Surface To Air System utilizes a wide variety of formational structures to attack modern defenses. One of the more eclectic formations we still use is the 2x1 Split Formation. This formation features the X, Y, and Z receivers split away from the box, although the Y receiver can also be attached to the box as a sniffer tight end and often is when we are in split backs. The H receiver and tailback remain in the backfield to form the split backs look.

A common formational variation that we will employ when in this set is our Bounce Motion Package. When we Bounce Motion we commonly bounce the H receiver away from the single side receiver towards the two receiver side. For the purpose of this chapter we assume that the Snag Concept will be the concept for the two receiver side of the formation (Diagram 79).

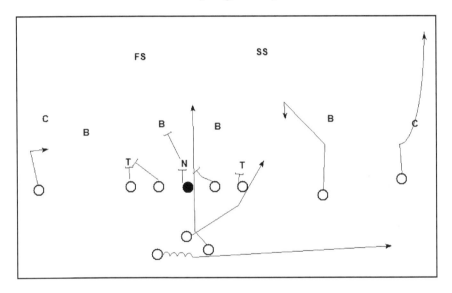

Diagram 79

The motion by the H receiver is done right before the snap of the ball and he should progress to just behind the tailback as the ball is snapped. This motion is designed to get him a running head start and to force the defense to either distort at the last moment or become outnumbered to the perimeter. In this example we are locking the inside zone and reading the Mike linebacker. We tell the quarterback if there is "color leaving the box" then he should hand the ball off because the defense is moving to equate numbers. If there is "no color leaving the box" then the defense allowed themselves to get outnumbered in the flat and the quarterback should pull the football and read the R2 for where to throw the football.

The next type of motion, still paired with the ubiquitous Snag Concept, we will look at is a motion we call Long Motion. This motion is very simple in that it simply trades a receiver from one side of the formation to the other. This can be to trade the formation from a 3x1 to a 2x2 set or a 2x2 set to a 3x1 set. In this diagram we are trading the formation from a 2x2 set to a 3x1 set and allowing the defense to decide whether to adjust or not. The quarterback will not snap the ball until the H receiver has made it to the general location he would normally align in for a 3x1 formation (Diagram 80).

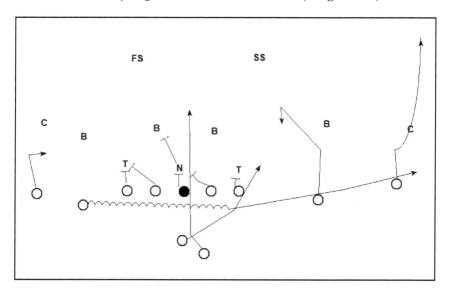

Diagram 80

Once again, the motion is designed to require the defense to make an adjustment or to become outnumbered to the 3x. This is also a locked RPO and the quarterback will once again read the Mike linebacker in the above diagram to determine if he should hand the ball off or throw it to the perimeter. The defense must add a player to the 3x1 side of the formation or else they are outnumbered. A play caller can elect to have this play be locked so the quarterback has a bit more time to read the play or he can design it unlocked to allow the quarterback to be a runner and place the defense in a greater amount of conflict.

A third type of motion we utilize in the Surface To Air System is the Jet Motion Package. The tailback is set to the right and the H receiver is motioning to the right and so this formational package simulate the Jet Sweep play very well. We want to distort the defense and get them moving only to realize we are actually running an interior run back to the direction the motion originated from (Diagram 81).

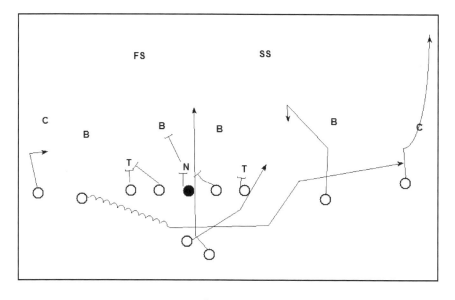

Diagram 81

This RPO, for simplicity in this writing, is also shown locked. All of the RPOs in this section could of course be taught as unlocked RPOs that are read all the way out. This motion is designed to get the defense moving fast horizontally after they have been hit with the Jet Sweep a few times. This is once again a "color or no color leaving the box" read for the quarterback and is very easy for him to read. The Flat Route by the H receiver pairs nicely with the motion as he is able to get up a big head of steam and outrun any player chasing him through the box. This is a great "go to play" when the defense chooses to play Cover 1 or Cover 0 and attempt to run with motioning receivers. There is a lot of traffic for the defender to navigate and a large number of built in "rubs" to stop defenders from completing their coverage assignments.

The next motion package is the Orbit Motion which is very similar to the Bounce motion except this one is designed from a 2x2 set (Diagram 82).

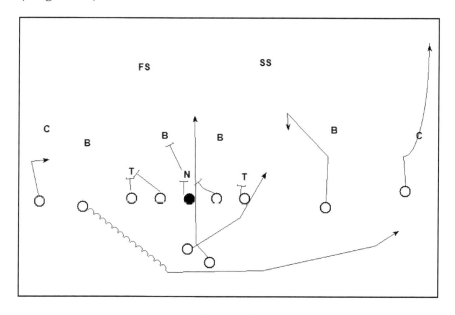

Diagram 82

The Bounce Motion was designed to have the H receiver next to the quarterback and then leave the box quickly. This motion features the H receiver aligned already in a 2x2 set and then executing the same motion as Bounce Motion but doing it from width. This enables the offense to force the defense to remain balanced until the last second but still has the advantage, like Bounce Motion, of keeping the motioning receiver away from defenders so they cannot man him up as easily. This RPO is locked and should remind the reader a great

108

deal of Bounce Motion simply being accomplished from a slightly different starting formational structure.

Another great way to distort the defense is through the use of motion involving the sniffer tight end. Over the past few seasons the Surface To Air System has become quite resourceful in utilizing the sniffer to do a wide variety of things for us. A great motion to use then is the Bulldog Motion Package which calls for the Y receiver to line up in a traditional split receiver position and then motion to his preordained sniffer alignment (Diagram 83).

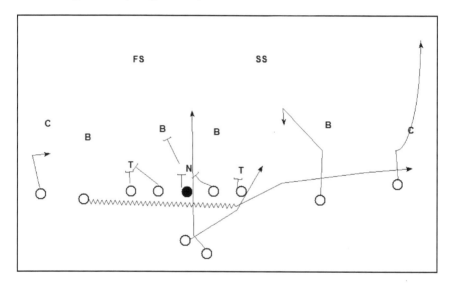

Diagram 83

This motion will often destroy coverage and blitz checks that the defense had in place. The defense will have a check for 2x2 and they will have a check for a sniffer set but they often do not like to check from one to the other in a pre-snap situation. This motion allows the offense to switch from one popular formational structure to another and to do so right before the ball is snapped. This change is very detrimental to the defense and keeps the quarterbacks "color or no color" leaving the box read very much intact. Once again for the sake of continuity and simplicity this RPO is shown locked but the play caller could elect to build this RPO locked or unlocked to suit his personal preference.

The Surface To Air System also, from time to time, wishes to line up in a 3x2 set to gauge the intentions of the defense. We have discussed previously that the 3x2 set often forces the defense to tip their hand and show what sort of pressure or coverage family they wish to utilize. The offense is able to gain an advantage by lining up in this formation and then forcing the defense to present their best answers.

However, the one drawback is that the quarterback must essentially be the between the tackles running back and this may not be what a coach wants to call on a consistent basis throughout the contest. A play caller may not want his quarterback running the ball so much, he may want to feature the tailback, or he may just favor the deception of two backs in the back field. Whatever the case, the Surface To Air System had to create a motion package that allowed the offense to feature a 3x2 formation but still get back into a one back formational set pre-snap. The answer for us is a motion known as our Cal Motion Package (Diagram 84).

This motion package features the tailback lining up in 3x2 set and then motioning back into the backfield and then taking his regularly signaled alignment and executing the run portion of the RPO that was called. Once again, this RPO could be locked or unlocked. This motioning style has the advantage that it forces the defense to play one sort of structure versus 3x2, and then morph pre-snap to defend a 3x1 structure all while maintaining RPO/option structure scrutiny inside its rules and checks. This is a large amount of information for the defense to process and they must be able to communicate these changes and adaptations very quickly or else the offense will have an inherent advantage.

The use of motion based RPOs is a new and exciting way to attack modern defenses with the Surface To Air System. These RPOs do not require major changes on the part of the offense they are quite simple to read and execute. What these plays accomplish is a massive and fairly natural distortion of the defense and places on the defense and enhance need to effectively communicate between their sideline and players on the field.

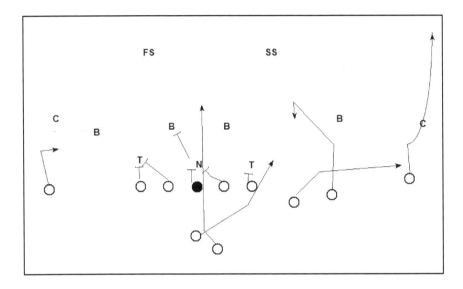

Diagram 84

The added stress that this places on the defense is a huge advantage to the offense. These motions are sometimes never used, used extensively, or on an ad hoc basis in a given week. It is up to the play caller to decipher which motions should be used and with what run and pass concepts so that they are of maximum use to the offense and maximum detriment to the defense. These plays serve as a useful and cutting edge extension of the basic RPOs that have made the Surface To Air System so successful over the past few seasons.

Snag Pivot Concept

We are now looking at a concept that we call a Snag/Pivot Concept. We've done stick, snag, and spot, which are all quick game concepts

111

that we can RPO. This is our Snag/Pivot Concept which is actually a drop back concept. When we utilize a drop back concept such as Snag/Pivot we are actually taking a three step drop and reading the secondary coverage from Deep to Shallow to Mid. This is not a quick game concept and it does not fit into the RPO world. However, because the route structure still involves the Snag Concept we will discuss it in this chapter.

When we call the Snag/Pivot Concept the second receiver is going to run the Snag Route. The difference is now, if that linebacker, the R2 attaches to him and takes his route away, he will pivot it back into the flat, and he will drag him with him. The number one receiver's going to run a seven step Dig Route, and now the quarterback can just process that out. If R2 bails and works back into the Dig Route path, we are going to throw that Pivot Route. If the R2 attaches to the pivot we're going to throw the Dig Route behind him. We will hold the hash safety by running the third receiver, in this case the tailback, on a vertical Seam Route and he will actually be the first read in a Deep to Shallow to Mid progression (Diagram 85).

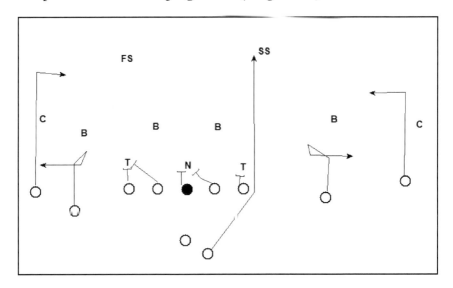

Diagram 85

We are actually going to mirror that concept on the back of the play and give the quarterback the same routes on the back side that he has front side. If he does not like the progression on the front side of the play he will simply play high to low on the back side of the formation.

This Snag/Pivot Concept is a great route structure but it is best served from a 3x1 set. When we call it from a 3x1 set everything's the same, except the number three receiver who is now the H receiver is going to run that locked seam route. He's going to outside release, bend it up there. That's how we're gonna take care of a safety who's trying to rob that Dig Route (Diagram 86).

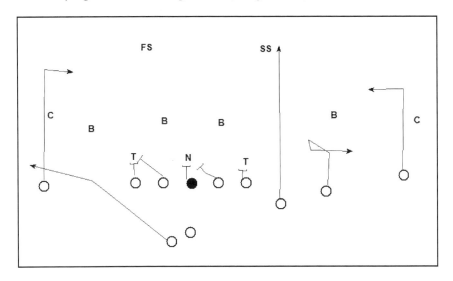

Diagram 86

So if that safety had come down, we'd just fire that to the Seam Route as fast as possible and punish him for peeling at the Dig Route. Obviously the Mike has to take the low seam and the safety's going to need to take the high seam. This will mean that we've got two defenders taken out with just one route. If they don't cover it, we throw it. If they do cover it, we can work back to our other two receivers. That's something you don't throw a lot, but when you are able to throw it out of trips, you get them into a situation where they've got to cover that vertical Seam Route and then it's much easier to play these other two routes.

The Snag/Pivot Concept is a great concept to call versus a wide variety of coverages. The Dig Route that always remains on the backside of the structure with some sort of flat running route is an easy check down for the quarterback if he doesn't like what is going on to the front side. This concept is a drop back portion of our offense but we have found a way to build the Snag Route into it with the extension of a Pivot Route to make the route all the more lethal. When defenses attach to the Snag Route it gives the receiver a way to get open or to drag his Dig Route running comrade into open grass.

Conclusion

The Stick, Snag, and Spot Concepts are all household concepts in the Surface To Air System. All of these concepts feature the Deep to shallow to mid-read progression and they are all very easy for the quarterback to read throughout the progression. These routes are malleable and can mutate through the use of formations or motions, as we discussed above at length, to make them lethal parts of our offensive package. The Snag Route can even be transitioned into a portion of our drop back passing scheme as well.

Every offense needs a "hang your hat" section of plays that are able to be replicated and transitional to a wide range of areas inside the offensive scheme. These concepts serve as the bedrock of the Surface To Air System quick passing attack. We attempt to build multiple plays around these simple reads. In essence, about two thirds of all of our quick passes have a triangular read built into them which is the basis for the Stick, Snag, and Spot Concepts. These plays have long served us well and will continue to be a major part of our offensive attack in terms of quick passes and RPOs for years to come.

Final Thoughts

This manual is the combined efforts of our entire team at Surface To Air System. We feel that this manual is a great way to spread our message about the game of football. At the tactical level the Surface To Air System is attempting to help football coaches to gain more 1st Downs and score more touchdowns. But at the strategic level the system is designed to make the game of football safer through our style of play and to help increase participation in the sport. We feel that when the game is spread out and avoids mass piles of humanity it is both safer and more fun.

We have fundamentally altered the way that we practice the game of football with a new structure we call GPS. The GPS, Game Practice System, is a game simulation style of practice that involves less contact and increased game sensitive repetitions in practice. We have also begun to utilize technology both in practice and on game nights to protect our athletes from injury and to make the game more enticing for the young people that play for us.

Our members are served by us on a monthly basis with live and interactive webinars that attempt to consult and troubleshoot issues that are members are experiencing. These sessions are also designed to expose our members to new and exciting tweaks and variations in the system that we wish to "push out" to them to make the system more lethal. We also feature webinars during the season for our members that support them every Sunday afternoon throughout the game planning and play calling process of the season. The chapters that we have selected for this manual are the best of the best lectures and discussions that we had throughout the year. These are ideas, plays, and trends that we felt most enabled our coaches to grow professionally and we wished to offer them to you as a non-member as well.

Far too often the trend in high school football has been to do less with more. The budgets of athletic department simply do not allow coaches to attend clinics across the country, go visit with college coaches, or spend the sort of time with their colleagues that is needed in order to perfect their craft. The webinars that we conduct throughout the season our attempt to fill the void that some of our members might have and being able to reach out across the country and network with coaches.

These webinars, obviously are led by myself, but they are participated in by a multitude of members across all four major time zones in the United States. In addition we have members from as far away as Europe, Asia, and South America. We have coaches throughout the United States and Canada who take part in these webinars on a monthly and weekly basis in order to improve their craft. It is our hope that these webinars expand the knowledge of the coaches in our system. As we stated previously, we are not looking to simply build a better mousetrap.

What we are attempting to do with this system is grow the game of football and expose it to a wider variety of people. It is our belief that into many corners of the United States and around the world the game is still a fundamentally smashmouth style of football. We are attempting to change this. We want to make the game more exciting, safer, and one that recruits more athletes onto football programs in the hope that more young men are exposed to high quality coaching by great mentors and great moral leaders.

As a young football coach I often travel across the country attempting to get college coaches to speak to me and show me the latest and most cutting-edge ideas in offense in football. We feel that this system now alleviates the need to travel across the country for so many of our members. What this manual, and the system overall, is also attempting to do is it's attempting to expose all the coaches that read our works or our members of our system to a common philosophical belief. We are an RPO based spread offense. But we utilize a wide variety of tweaks and variations in order to acquire first downs and score touchdowns. We will play with or without a tight end. We will line up in empty or we will line up under Center. We will go from a very quick Tempo set or we will slow the game down into a four-minute offense. We discuss a wide variety of things inside our system from the Red Zone, to how we come out of our own end zone, two are down and distance philosophies, to how we practice and Coach our kids.

Our members even discuss things such as weight training and offseason development. It is our hope that these manuals become a lasting and indelible part of what our system is attempting to accomplish. We have a diverse group of members spread out throughout the United States and the world to offer their viewpoints and their thoughts about how to make the game of football better each and every time we meet.

As all of these coaches come together we feel like we are essentially all adding ingredients to a large. As each member contributes more and add more of their own thoughts and viewpoints to this to become better and better tasting. This manual is just another attempt to accomplish this. We are attempting to offer some of the best things we have discussed throughout the year as a system to you, the non-member, in an attempt to expand upon some of our ideas and expose them to the public at large. It is our hope that several you reading this work will eventually decide to be members of our fraternity.

Whether you decide to join our fraternity or the purchase of this manual is just a small foray into our system we hope that the information that we have provided you is useful to you and helps you grow inside the game of football. It is our fervent hope that everything we do as a system contributes not just to each member's ability to score more points and win more games but that it also helps to make the game of football better. It is our desire that the game of football continues to grow and continues to expand and continues to teach the life lessons that we feel they teach on a daily basis to young men not only throughout the United States but throughout the world. The game of football is one of the last great bastions of teamwork, accountability, structure, and hard work based success that young people are taught in our culture today.

We feel that without the game of football young men would be lacking in motivation, Drive, work ethic, and a general degree of accountability that is hard to teach in our regular culture throughout its day-to-day progression. Therefore, our system is designed to not only help our members but to expand the game of football. We hope that this manual has been useful to you and that you have learn some useful and practical tips in how to make your own football team better. We understand that this is a results-driven culture that we live in. We know that good coaches must win games in order to keep their positions in our high-paced and results-driven Society. We hope that this manual helps you to score more points and win more games. And we also hope that as you are scoring points and winning games you continue to teach the valuable life lessons to young man that cannot and should not be taught anywhere other than on the Gridiron!

ABOUT THE AUTHOR

Rich Hargitt has been a football coach since 1999. He has served as a head football coach and offensive coordinator at the high school level in Illinois, Indiana, North Carolina, and South Carolina. In 2010, he earned a Master's of Arts Degree in Physical Education with Coaching Specialization from Ball State University. Hargitt's teams have utilized the Air Raid Offense to upset several quality teams and the offense has produced school record holders in rushing and passing. Coach Hargitt's first Air Raid Quarterback, Mitch Niekamp, holds several college records at Illinois College and is currently a starting Quarterback in Europe's professional leagues. He previously contributed to a six-part video series on the Spread Wing-T offense for American Football Monthly and has been published numerous times in coaching journals on the Air Raid Offense. He has spoken for both the Nike Coach of the Clinics and the Glazier Clinics about the Air Raid Offense.

His first book 101 Shotgun Wing-T Plays was published by Coaches Choice in 2012. Coach Hargitt's second book 101 Air Raid Plays was published by Coaches Choice in 2013. Hargitt's third book, Coaching the Air Raid Offense, was published in 2014. Hargitt's fourth and fifth books, Packaging Plays in the Air Raid Offense and Play Calling for the Air Raid Offense, were released in January of 2015. The 6th book in the Hargitt collection, Coaching the RPO Offense, was released in 2016. The 7th work by Hargitt, 101 RPO Plays, was released in 2017. Coach Hargitt has also collaborated with Coaches Choice on a series of DVDs detailing the Air Raid Offense. Hargitt brought the Air Raid Offense to Nation Ford High School in 2011 where he helped lead the Falcons to their first non-losing season, first AAA Region victory, first AAA Playoff berth, and first AAA Playoff victory. In 2012, Hargitt's offense broke the school single game and single season offensive records for passing yards, touchdowns, and points scored. Also in 2012, Hargitt helped lead Nation Ford HS to the AAAA playoffs for the first time in school history.

In 2013, Hargitt helped lead the Ashbrook Greenwave to the second round of NCHSAA AAA playoffs and a 9-4 overall record. He is currently the Assistant Head Coach/Offensive Coordinator at Eastside HS in Taylors, SC. In 2015 Hargitt's offense achieved a statewide Top 10 ranking, averaged 383 yards per game (231 passing, 152 rushing), finished ranked in the Top 10 of the state and Top 5 of AAA in passing, achieved 2nd non-losing season in 13 years. In 2016 the offense improved even further as the team advanced to the SCHSL AAAA Playoffs. In addition, the offense averaged 488 yards per game (286 passing, 202 rushing) and 41 points per game in the regular season and finished the season in AAAA ranked 4th in rushing (2,127 yards), 3rd in rushing touchdowns (27), 1st in passing (3,311 yards), 1st in yards passing per game (301), 1st in pass completions (257), 1st in pass attempts (365), 1st in passing touchdowns (37), 1st in completion percentage (70%), 1st in touchdowns scored (65), 1st in scoring (453), 1st in PATs made (53) and 1st in total yardage from scrimmage (5,438 yards). The offense also led the State of South Carolina in Total Yardage from Scrimmage (5,438 yards).

The 2016 offense also featured a quarterback that completed the 3rd most passes in a game and 3rd most touchdown passes in a single game in state history. In addition, the offense featured a receiver that the 4th most passes in a single game and 6th most passes in a season in state history. Hargitt's 2017 Southside HS team broke the school single game passing record and the school single season passing record. In addition, the offense finished the regular season ranked in AAA 6th in rushing (1082 yards), 1st in passing yards (2328 yards), 1st in completions (192), 1st in pass attempts (318), 1st in passing touchdowns (21), and 3rd in completion percentage (60%). Hargitt led the tigers to a 7 point per game improvement from the year before he arrived and helped lead the Tigers to the SCHSL AAA playoffs.

In the spring of 2018 Hargitt accepted the Head Football position at Emmett High School in Emmett, Idaho. Since 2011, Hargitt's teams have amassed 28, 566 total yards with 17,248 of those yards coming through the air and 11, 317 yards on the ground. Hargitt resides in Middleton, Idaho with his wife Lisa and their sons Griffin and Graham.

Want to learn more about The Surface to Air System?

Check out SurfaceToAirSystem.com

OR

Contact Rich Hargitt at

SurfaceToAirSystem.com/Contact

Made in the USA
Middletown, DE
23 November 2018